Electric Slide

Colorful Socks

by Knit Picks

Photography by Elizabeth LePage
& Regan Nishikawa
Graphic Design by Lee Meredith
Content Direction by Stacey Winklepleck
Creative Direction by Hillary Elliott

Printed in the United States of America
First Printing, 2022

ISBN 978-1-62767-323-5

Versa Press, Inc.

800-447-7829
www.versapress.com

CONTENTS

Ballantyre *by Amy Snell*   8

Bend Lines *by Mone Dräger*   14

Dashing *by Sarah Dobbins*   20

Delicate *by Aimee Sher*   24

Emergent Properties *by Carolyn Lisle*   28

Extra Frosting *by Brenda K.B. Anderson*   34

Flowering Meadow *by Mone Dräger*   38

Interlink *by Sandi Rosner*   44

Jive *by Katie Noseworthy*   **48**

Liana *by Aud Bergo*   **54**

Nouveau *by Katy Banks*   **58**

Pistachio *by Lauren Rose*   **64**

Sparkling Crystals *by Aud Bergo*   **70**

Three Steps Forward *by Paula Niskasaari*   **76**

Topaz *by Nancy Vandivert*   **80**

Valensole *by Margaret Stauffacher*   **86**

Glossary   **94**

BALLANTYRE
by Amy Snell

FINISHED MEASUREMENTS
6.75 (7.25, 8.75)" foot circumference ×
8 (9, 10)" foot length, meant to be worn
with approx 10% negative ease

YARN
Hawthorne™ (fingering weight, 80%
Fine Superwash Highland Wool, 20%
Polyamide (Nylon); 357 yards/100g):
Abernathy 26863, 1 (1, 2) hank(s)

NEEDLES
US 2 (2.75mm) DPNs or two circular
needles for two circulars technique or
32" or longer circular needles for Magic
Loop technique, or size to obtain gauge

US 1 (2.25mm) DPNs or two circular
needles for two circulars technique or
32" or longer circular needles for Magic
Loop technique, or one size smaller
than size used to obtain gauge

NOTIONS
Yarn Needle
Stitch Markers

GAUGE
28 sts and 40 rnds = 4" in Stockinette
Stitch in the round, blocked
40 sts and 40 rnds= 4" in Foot Chart
Stitch in the round, blocked
40 sts and 40 rnds= 4" in Leg Chart
Stitch in the round, blocked

For pattern support, contact deviousknitter@gmail.com

Ballantyre

Notes:

The twists and turns of these intricate-looking socks are a tribute to the meandering paths and brooks that crisscross the Irish countryside, where footbridges and one-lane roads are the most common thoroughfares and meandering sheep may be the most likely cause of a traffic jam.

Ballantyre combines two unusual cables, neither of which is formed in a true cable manner. Instead, these motifs make interesting use of increases, decreases, slipped stitches, and PSSOs. The two patterns—one larger, one smaller—alternate to form an eye-catching all-over texture. Ballantyre is knit toe-up, with a flap-and-gusset heel that looks traditional but is accomplished in the reverse manner from most flap-and-gusset heels.

The Sl3 WYIF in the Leg Stitch Pattern will restrict the stretch of the fabric; to avoid making the leg of the socks too tight, spread the slipped sts out on the right needle when making the next st.

Pattern is written for two needles (Instep and Sole); if using DPNs divide stitches between more needles as needed.

Chart is worked in the round; read each chart row from right to left as a RS row.

Bind 3 (Bind one slipped stitch over three)
Sl1 WYIB, K1, YO, K1, PSSO the 3 subsequent sts.

Foot Stitch Pattern — Sizes 6.75 (-, 8.75)" (in the round over a multiple of 12 sts plus 7)
Rnd 1: P2, K3, P2, (K2, P2, K2, P1, K3, P2) 2 (-, 3) times.
Rnd 2: P2, Bind 3, P2, (K2, P2, K2, P1, Bind 3, P2) 2 (-, 3) times.
Rnds 3–4: Rep Rnd 1.
Rep Rnds 1–4 for pattern.

Foot Stitch Pattern — Size 7.25" (in the round over a multiple of 10 sts plus 5)
Rnd 1: P1, K3, P1, *(K2, P1) two times, K3, P1; rep from * two more times.
Rnd 2: P1, Bind 3, P1, *(K2, P1) two times, Bind 3, P1; rep from * two more times.
Rnds 3–4: Rep Rnd 1.
Rep Rnds 1–4 for pattern.

Leg Stitch Pattern — Sizes 6.75 (-, 8.75)" (in the round beginning with a multiple of 22 sts)
Rnd 1: *P2, K3, P2, K5, (P2, K3) two times; rep from * 2 (-, 3) times.
Rnd 2: (P2, Bind 3, P2, K2, [K1, YO, K1] in 1 st, K2, P2, Bind 3, P2, Sl3 WYIF) 3 (-, 4) times. 6 (-, 8) sts inc.
Rnds 3–5: (P2, K3, P2, K7, P2, K3, P2, Sl3 WYIF) 3 (-, 4) times.
Rnd 6: (P2, Bind 3, P2, K2, CDD, K2, P2, Bind 3, P2, Sl3 WYIF) 3 (-, 4) times. 6 (-, 8) sts dec.
Rnd 7: *P2, K3, P2, K5, (P2, K3) two times; rep from * 2 (-, 3) more times.
Rnd 8: (P2, K3, P2, K1, CDD, K1, P2, K3, P2, K1, [K1, YO, K1] in 1 st, K1) 3 (-, 4) times.

Rnd 9: *(P2, K3) three times, P2, K5; rep from * 2 (3) more times.
Rnd 10: (P2, Bind 3, P2, Sl3 WYIF, P2, Bind 3, P2, K2, [K1, YO, K1] in 1 st, K2) 3 (-, 4) times. 6 (-, 8) sts inc.
Rnds 11–13: (P2, K3, P2, Sl3 WYIF, P2, K3, P2, K7) 3 (-, 4) times.
Rnd 14: (P2, Bind 3, P2, Sl3 WYIF, P2, Bind 3, P2, K2, CDD, K2) 3 (-, 4) times. 6 (-, 8) sts dec.
Rnd 15: Rep Rnd 9.
Rnd 16: (P2, K3, P2, K1, [K1, YO, K1] in 1 st, K1, P2, K3, P2, K1, CDD, K1) 3 (-, 4) times.
Rep Rnds 1–16 for pattern.

Leg Stitch Pattern — Size 7.25" (in the round beginning with a multiple of 18 sts)
Rnd 1: *P1, K3, P1, K5, (P1, K3) two times; rep from * three more times.
Rnd 2: (P1, Bind 3, P1, K2, [K1, YO, K1] in 1 st, K2, P1, Bind 3, P1, Sl3 WYIF) four times. 8 sts inc.
Rnds 3–5: (P1, K3, P1, K7, P1, K3, P1, Sl3 WYIF) four times.
Rnd 6: (P1, Bind 3, P1, K2, CDD, K2, P1, Bind 3, P1, Sl3 WYIF) four times. 8 sts dec.
Rnd 7: *P1, K3, P1, K5, (P1, K3) two times; rep from * three more times.
Rnd 8: (P1, K3, P1, K1, CDD, K1, P1, K3, P1, K1, [K1, YO, K1] in 1 st, K1) four times.
Rnd 9: *(P1, K3) three times, P1, K5; rep from * three more times.
Rnd 10: (P1, Bind 3, P1, Sl3 WYIF, P1, Bind 3, P1, K2, [K1, YO, K1] in 1 st, K2) four times. 8 sts inc.
Rnds 11–13: (P1, K3, P1, Sl3 WYIF, P1, K3, P1, K7) four times.
Rnd 14: (P1, Bind 3, P1, Sl3 WYIF, P1, Bind 3, P1, K2, CDD, K2) four times. 8 sts dec.
Rnd 15: Rep Rnd 9.
Rnd 16: (P1, K3, P1, K1, [K1, YO, K1] in 1 st, K1, P1, K3, P1, K1, CDD, K1) four times.
Rep Rnds 1–16 for pattern.

DIRECTIONS

Toe
Using Judy's Magic Cast On, CO 24 (28, 32) sts, 12 (14, 16) each on instep and sole needles. PM for BOR.
Rnd 1: K all.
Rnd 2: Instep Needle—K1, KFB, K to last 3 sts, KFB, K2; Sole Needle—K1, KFB, K to last 3 sts, KFB, K2. 2 sts inc each needle; 4 sts inc total.
Rep Rnds 1–2 another 5 (5, 7) times. 48 (52, 64) sts.

Foot
Work St st for 1".

Size 6.75" Only
Setup Rnd: Instep Needle—(K2, M1, K3, M1, K3, M1) three times; Sole Needle—K to end. 57 sts.

Size 7.25" Only

Setup Rnd: Instep Needle—*K2, (M1, K3) two times, M1, K2, M1, K3, M1; rep from * once more; Sole Needle—K to end. 62 sts.

Size 8.75" Only

Setup Rnd: Instep Needle—*K2, M1, (K3, M1) five times; rep from * once more; Sole Needle—K to end. 76 sts.

Resume All Sizes

Next Rnd: Instep Needle—K1 (0, 0), work Foot Stitch Pattern from appropriate size chart or written instructions, K1 (0, 0); Sole Needle—K to end.

Cont as established until foot measures 4.25 (4.75, 5)" from CO.

Gusset

Cont working Instep Needle in established pattern. AT THE SAME TIME, inc for gusset on Sole Needle only, as follows.

Rnd 1: K1, PM, M1R, K to last st, M1L, PM, K1. 2 sts inc.

Rnd 2: K all.

Rnd 3: K1, M1R, (K to M, SM) two times, K to last st, M1L, K1. 2 sts inc.

Rnd 4: K all.

Rep Rnds 3-4 another 10 (12, 15) times. 81 (90, 110) sts.

Rep Rnd 3 once more. 83 (92, 112) sts.

Next Rnd: K1, (K2, M1R) 6 (6, 7) times, K1 (2, 3), SM, K to M, SM, (K2, M1R) 6 (6, 7) times, K2 (3, 4). 12 (12, 14) sts inc.

Heel Turn

Heel Turn is worked over center 24 (26, 32) sts between Ms on Sole Needle

Short Row 1 (RS): Instep Needle—work as established; Sole Needle—K to M, SM, K to 2 sts before M, W&T.

Short Row 2 (WS): P to 2 sts before M, W&T.

Short Row 3: K to 3 sts before M, W&T.

Short Row 4: P to 3 sts before M, W&T.

Short Row 5: K to 4 sts before M, W&T.

Short Row 6: P to 4 sts before the M, W&T.

Cont working short rows as established, adding 1 to the number of sts before M on each rep, until 7 (8, 9) sts are on each side and 10 (10, 14) remain unwrapped in center.

Next Short Row (RS): K to last 2 sts, lifting each wrap and knitting it tog with its wrapped st, SSK final wrapped st with remaining st, turn. 1 st dec.

Next Short Row (WS): Sl1 WYIF, P to last 2 sts, lifting each wrap and purling it tog with its wrapped st, P2tog final wrapped st with remaining st, turn. 1 st dec.

Heel Flap

Cont working only on Sole Needle.

Row 1 (RS): Sl1 WYIB, (K1, Sl1 WYIB) to 1 st before M, remove M, SSK, turn. 1 st dec.

Row 2: (WS): Sl1 WYIF, P to 1 st before M, remove M, P2tog, turn. 1 st dec.

Row 3: Sl1 WYIB, (K1, Sl1 WYIB) to 1 st before gap, SSK, turn. 1 st dec.

Row 4: Sl1 WYIF, P to 1 st before gap, P2tog, turn. 1 st dec.

Rep Rows 3-4 until all but 1 gusset st on each side have been consumed, ending on a WS row, turn.

Next Row (RS): (Sl1 WYIB, K1) to 1 st before gap (last 2 sts), SSK. 58 (63, 77) sts.

Leg

Resume working in the rnd. Instep Needle (first needle) is now Front Needle and Sole Needle (second needle) is now Back Needle.

Setup Rnd: Front Needle—Resume working Foot Stitch Pattern as established; Back Needle—K2tog, K to end. 57 (62, 76) sts.

If Rnd 2 of Foot Stitch Pattern was just worked, skip Next Rnd.

Next Rnd: Front Needle—work Foot Stitch Pattern as established; Back Needle—K to end.

Cont as established if applicable until Rnd 2 of Foot Stitch Pattern has been completed.

Size 6.75" Only

Next Rnd: Front Needle—work Rnd 3 of Foot Stitch Pattern; Back Needle—(K2, M1, K3, M1, K2, M1, K2, M1, K2, M1) two times, K2, M1. 11 sts inc; 68 sts total.

Next Rnd: K1 then move this st over to Back Needle, making the next st the new BOR; P2, K3, P2, K5, P2, K3, P2, K1, CDD, K1, *P2, K3, P2, K5, (P2, K3) two times; rep from * once more. 2 sts dec; 66 sts.

Size 7.25" Only

Next Rnd: Front Needle—work Rnd 3 of Foot Stitch Pattern; Back Needle—(K2, M1) twelve times, K2. 12 sts inc; 74 sts total.

Next Rnd: K1 then move this st over to Back Needle, making this the new BOR; P1, K3, P1, K5, P1, K3, P1, K1, CDD, K1, (P1, K3, P1, K5, P1, K3, P1, K3) three times. 2 sts dec; 72 sts.

Size 8.75" Only

Next Rnd: Front Needle—work Rnd 3 of Foot Stitch Pattern; Back Needle—(K3, M1, K2, M1, K2, M1, K2, M1, K2, M1) twice, K3, M1, K2, M1, K2, M1, K2, M1, K2. 14 sts inc; 90 sts total.

Next Rnd: K1 then move this st over to Back Needle, making this the new BOR; P2, K3, P2, K5, P2, K3, P2, K1, CDD, K1, *P2, K3, P2, K5, (P2, K3) two times; rep from * two more times. 88 sts.

Resume All Sizes

Next Rnd: Work Leg Stitch Pattern from appropriate size chart or written instructions.

Cont as established until leg is approx 6" from heel turn, or to desired height.

Cuff

With smaller needles, work 1x1 Rib for 1".

BO using Stretchy Bind Off.

Second Sock

Make second sock same as first.

Finishing

Weave in ends, wash, and block as desired.

Foot Chart, 6.75 (-, 8.75)" sizes

19 18 17 16 15 14 13 12 11 10 9 8 7 6 5 4 3 2 1

4
3
2
1

Foot Chart, - (7.25, -)" size

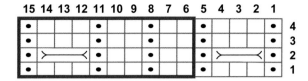

15 14 13 12 11 10 9 8 7 6 5 4 3 2 1

4
3
2
1

Leg Setup, 6.75 (-, 8.75)" sizes

44 43 42 41 40 39 38 37 36 35 34 33 32 31 30 29 28 27 26 25 24 23 22 21 20 19 18 17 16 15 14 13 12 11 10 9 8 7 6 5 4 3 2 1

0

Leg Setup, - (7.25, -)" size

36 35 34 33 32 31 30 29 28 27 26 25 24 23 22 21 20 19 18 17 16 15 14 13 12 11 10 9 8 7 6 5 4 3 2 1

0

LEGEND

No Stitch
Placeholder—no stitch made

Knit Stitch

Purl Stitch

Sl WYIF
Slip stitch purl-wise, with yarn in front

CDD
Slip first and second stitches together as if to K2tog;
knit 1 stitch; pass 2 slipped stitches over the knit stitch

Bind 3
Sl1 WYIB, K1, YO, K1, pass slipped st over
the 3 subsequent stitches

K-YO-K
(Knit 1, Yarn Over, Knit 1) into 1 stitch

Pattern Repeat

Leg Chart, - (7.25, -)" size

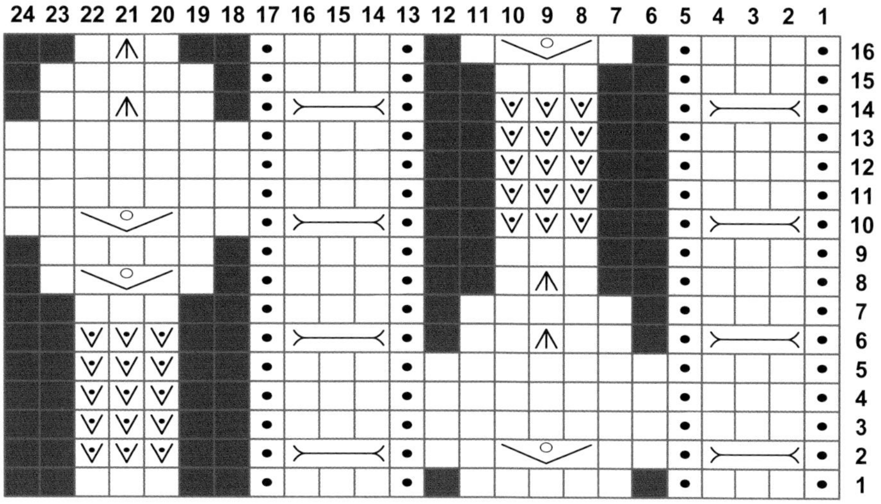

Leg Chart, 6.75 (-, 8.75)" sizes

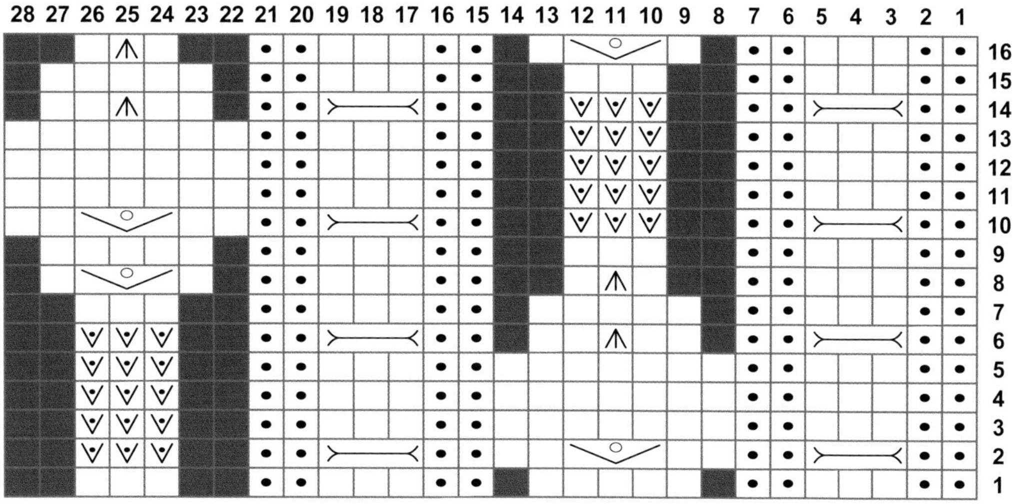

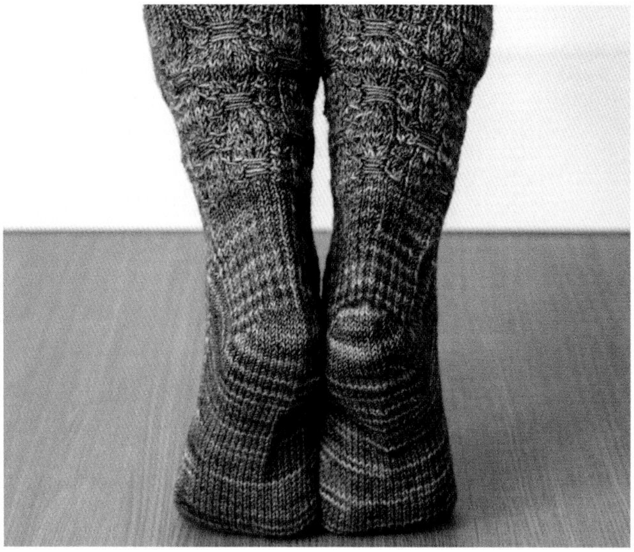

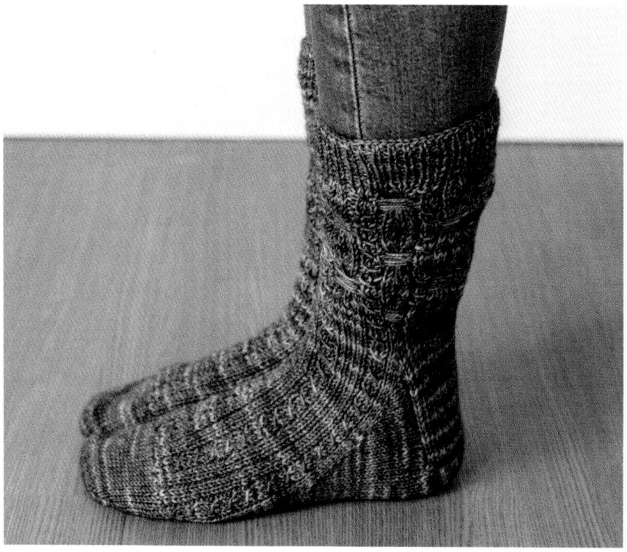

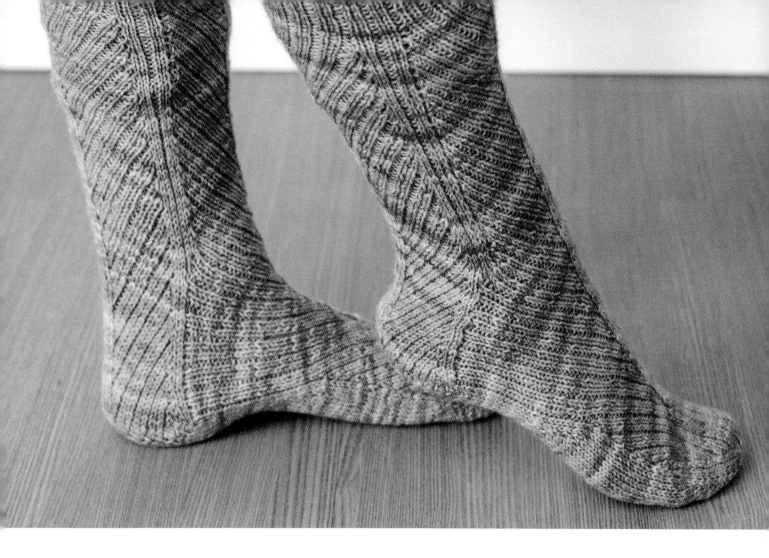

BEND LINES
by Mone Dräger

FINISHED MEASUREMENTS

7 (8.5)″ circumference × 6.5″ leg length to heel, foot length is customizable; meant to be worn with approx 10% negative ease

YARN

Muse™ Hand Painted Sock Yarn (fingering weight, 75% Superwash Merino Wool, 25% Nylon; 423 yards/100g): Pizzazz 28806, 1 hank

NEEDLES

US 2 (2.75mm) DPNs or two circular needles for two circulars technique or 32″ or longer circular needles for Magic Loop technique, or size to obtain gauge

NOTIONS

Yarn Needle
Stitch Markers
Scrap Yarn or Stitch Holder (optional)

GAUGE

34 sts and 42 rnds = 4″ in Stockinette Stitch in the round, blocked
34 sts and 42 rnds = 4″ in Slanted 2x1 Rib in the round, blocked (note that this is approximate due to the amount of stretch in the ribbing)

For pattern support, contact mone.draeger@web.de

Bend Lines

Notes:

Ribbing patterns are perfect for socks because they provide a snug yet comfortable fit. Bend Lines socks spice up plain ribbing with cleverly placed decreases and increases to create diagonal stripes. The socks are worked with an unconventional gusset shaping to keep the knitting interesting.

The socks are knit cuff down almost entirely in 2x1 ribbing with heel flap and gusset. The gusset decreases are done on the instep (arch shaped). The placement of decreases and increases creates diagonal stripes going toward the middle of the front and back of the leg. The ribbing stitch pattern is continued onto the heel flap and the toe.

Charts are worked both in the round and flat. When working chart in the round, read each chart row from right to left as a RS row; when working chart flat, read RS rows (even numbers) from right to left, and WS rows (odd numbers) from left to right.

2x1 Rib (in the round over a multiple of 3 sts)
Rnd 1: (K2, P1) to end of rnd.
Rep Rnd 1 for pattern.
The rib pattern may start and end in different positions. The pattern uses the term 'work in established rib pattern', which means that all K sts from the previous rnd are worked as K sts and all P sts from the previous rnd are worked P sts.

M1PL (Make 1 Purl Left)
Pick up bar of yarn between needles from the front with LH needle, P newly picked up st through the back loop.

M1PR (Make 1 Purl Right)
Pick up bar of yarn between needles from the back with LH needle, P newly picked up st through the front loop.

Leg Pattern (in the round over a multiple of 30 (36) sts)
Rnd 1: K2, M1L, (P1, K2) 3 (4) times, K2tog, K1, P1, K1, SSK, (K2, P1) 3 (4) times, M1R, K2, P1.
Rnd 2: K3, (P1, K2) 3 (4) times, K2, P1, K2, (P1, K2) 3 (4) times, K3, P1.
Rnd 3: K2, M1L, (K1, P1, K1) 3 (4) times, K2tog, K1, P1, K1, SSK, (K1, P1, K1) 3 (4) times, M1R, K2, P1.
Rnd 4: K3, (K1, P1, K1) 3 (4) times, K2, P1, K2, (K1, P1, K1) 3 (4) times, K3, P1.
Rnd 5: K2, M1PL, (K2, P1) 3 (4) times, K2tog, K1, P1, K1, SSK, (P1, K2) 3 (4) times, M1PR, K2, P1.
Rnd 6: K2, P1, (K2, P1) 3 (4) times, K2, P1, K2, (P1, K2) 3 (4) times, P1, K2, P1.
Rep Rnds 1–6 for pattern.

Heel Flap Pattern (flat over 31 (37) sts)
Row 1 (WS): Sl1 WYIF, P2, K1, (P2, K1) 3 (4) times, P2, K1, P2, (K1, P2) 3 (4) times, K1, P3.
Row 2 (RS): Sl1 WYIB, K2, M1L, (P1, K2) 3 (4) times, K2tog, K1, P1, K1, SSK, (K2, P1) 3 (4) times, M1R, K3.
Row 3: Sl1 WYIF, P3, (K1, P2) 3 (4) times, K2, P1, K2, (P2, K1) 3 (4) times, P4.
Row 4: Sl1 WYIB, K2, M1L, (K1, P1, K1) 3 (4) times, K2tog, K1,

P1, K1, SSK, (K1, P1, K1) 3 (4) times, M1R, K3.
Row 5: Sl1 WYIF, P3, (P1, K1, P1) 3 (4) times, P2, K1, P2, (P1, K1, P1) 3 (4) times, P4.
Row 6: Sl1 WYIB, K2, M1PL, (K2, P1) 3 (4) times, K2tog, K1, P1, K1, SSK, (P1, K2) 3 (4) times, M1PR, K3.
Rep Rnds 1–6 for pattern.

Gusset & Arch Pattern (in the round beginning with 61 (67) sts)
Rnd 1: (P1, K2) 9 (10) times, K2tog, K1, P1, K1, SSK, (K2, P1) 9 (10) times. 59 (65) sts.
Rnd 2: (P1, K2) 9 (10) times, K2, P1, K2, (K2, P1) 9 (10) times.
Rnd 3: (P1, K2) four times, P1, K1, (K1, P1, K1) 4 (5) times, K2tog, K1, P1, K1, SSK, (K1, P1, K1) 4 (5) times, K1, (P1, K2) four times, P1. 57 (63) sts.
Rnd 4: (P1, K2) four times, P1, K1, (K1, P1, K1) 4 (5) times, K2, P1, K2, (K1, P1, K1) 4 (5) times, K1, (P1, K2) four times, P1.
Rnd 5: (P1, K2) four times, P1, (K2, P1) 4 (5) times, K2tog, K1, P1, K1, SSK, (P1, K2) 4 (5) times, (P1, K2) four times, P1. 55 (61) sts.
Rnd 6: (P1, K2) four times, P1, (K2, P1) 4 (5) times, K2, P1, K2, (P1, K2) 4 (5) times, (P1, K2) four times, P1.
Rnd 7: (P1, K2) 8 (9) times, K2tog, K1, P1, K1, SSK, (K2, P1) 8 (9) times. 53 (59) sts.
Rnd 8: (P1, K2) 8 (9) times, K2, P1, K2, (K2, P1) 8 (9) times.
Rnd 9: (P1, K2) three times, P1, K1, (K1, P1, K1) 4 (5) times, K2tog, K1, P1, K1, SSK, (K1, P1, K1) 4 (5) times, K1, (P1, K2) three times, P1. 51 (57) sts.
Rnd 10: (P1, K2) three times, P1, K1, (K1, P1, K1) 4 (5) times, K2, P1, K2, (K1, P1, K1) 4 (5) times, K1, (P1, K2) three times, P1.
Rnd 11: (P1, K2) three times, P1, (K2, P1) 4 (5) times, K2tog, K1, P1, K1, SSK, (P1, K2) 4 (5) times, (P1, K2) three times, P1. 49 (55) sts.
Rnd 12: (P1, K2) three times, P1, (K2, P1) 4 (5) times, K2, P1, K2, (P1, K2) 4 (5) times, (P1, K2) three times, P1.
Rnd 13: (P1, K2) 7 (8) times, K2tog, K1, P1, K1, SSK, (K2, P1) 7 (8) times. 47 (53) sts.
Rnd 14: (P1, K2) 7 (8) times, K2, P1, K2, (K2, P1) 7 (8).
Rnd 15: (P1, K2) two times, P1, K1, (K1, P1, K1) 4 (5) times, K2tog, K1, P1, K1, SSK, (K1, P1, K1) 4 (5) times, K1, (P1, K2) two times, P1. 45 (51) sts.
Rnd 16: (P1, K2) two times, P1, K1, (K1, P1, K1) 4 (5) times, K2, P1, K2, (K1, P1, K1) 4 (5) times, K1, (P1, K2) two times, P1.
Rnd 17: (P1, K2) two times, P1, (K2, P1) 4 (5) times, K2tog, K1, P1, K1, SSK, (P1, K2) 4 (5) times, (P1, K2) two times, P1. 43 (49) sts.
Rnd 18: (P1, K2) two times, P1, (K2, P1) 4 (5) times, K2, P1, K2, (P1, K2) 4 (5) times, (P1, K2) two times, P1.
Rnd 19: (P1, K2) 6 (7) times, K2tog, K1, P1, K1, SSK, (K2, P1) 6 (7) times. 41 (47) sts.
Rnd 20: (P1, K2) 6 (7) times, K2, P1, K2, (K2, P1) 6 (7) times.
Rnd 21: P1, K2, P1, K1, (K1, P1, K1) 4 (5) times, K2tog, K1, P1, K1, SSK, (K1, P1, K1) 4 (5) times, K1, P1, K2, P1. 39 (45) sts.
Rnd 22: P1, K2, P1, K1, (K1, P1, K1) 4 (5) times, K2, P1, K2, (K1, P1, K1) 4 (5) times, K1, P1, K2, P1.
Rnd 23: P1, K2, P1, (K2, P1) 4 (5) times, K2tog, K1, P1, K1, SSK, (P1, K2) 4 (5) times, P1, K2, P1. 37 (43) sts.

Rnd 24: P1, K2, P1, (K2, P1) 4 (5) times, K2, P1, K2, (P1, K2) 4 (5) times, P1, K2, P1.

Rnd 25: (P1, K2) 5 (6) times, K2tog, K1, P1, K1, SSK, (K2, P1) 5 (6) times. 35 (41) sts.

Rnd 26: (P1, K2) 5 (6) times, K2, P1, K2, (K2, P1) 5 (6) times.

Rnd 27: P1, K1, (K1, P1, K1) 4 (5) times, K2tog, K1, P1, K1, SSK, (K1, P1, K1) 4 (5) times, K1, P1. 33 (39) sts.

Rnd 28: P1, K1, (K1, P1, K1) 4 (5) times, K2, P1, K2, (K1, P1, K1) 4 (5) times, K1, P1.

Rnd 29: P1, (K2, P1) 4 (5) times, K2tog, K1, P1, K1, SSK, (P1, K2) 4 (5) times, P1. 31 (37) sts.

Rnd 30: P1, (K2, P1) 4 (5) times, K2, P1, K2, (P1, K2) 4 (5) times, P1.

Instep Pattern (in the rnd over a multiple of 31 (37) sts)

Rnd 1: M1L, (P1, K2) 4 (5) times, K2tog, K1, P1, K1, SSK, (K2, P1) 4 (5) times, M1R.

Rnd 2: K1, (P1, K2) 4 (5) times, K2, P1, K2, (K2, P1) 4 (5) times, K1.

Rnd 3: M1L, (K1, P1, K1) 4 (5) times, K2tog, K1, P1, K1, SSK, (K1, P1, K1) 4 (5) times, M1R.

Rnd 4: K1, (K1, P1, K1) 4 (5) times, K2, P1, K2, (K1, P1, K1) 4 (5) times, K1.

Rnd 5: M1PL, (K2, P1) 4 (5) times, K2tog, K1, P1, K1, SSK, (P1, K2) 4 (5) times, M1PR.

Rnd 6: P1, (K2, P1) 4 (5) times, K2, P1, K2, (P1, K2) 4 (5) times, P1.

Rep Rnds 1–6 for pattern.

DIRECTIONS

Cuff

Using your choice of stretchy cast on method, CO 60 (72) sts. Join to work in the rnd, being careful not to twist sts; PM for BOR.

Work 2x1 Rib for 16 rnds.

Leg

Work Leg Pattern from chart or written instructions twice around leg. Work Rnds 1–6 eight times, then rep Rnds 1–5 once more.

Heel Flap

Heel flap is worked back and forth in rows over the last 31 (37) sts of rnd; hold remaining 29 (35) sts for instep either on working needles or transfer to st holder or scrap yarn if preferred.

Turn work so that WS is facing and work Heel Flap Pattern from chart or written instructions. Work Rows 1–6 five times.

Heel Turn

Short Row 1 (WS): P18 (22), P2tog, P1, turn.
Short Row 2 (RS): Sl1 WYIB, K6 (8), SSK, K1, turn.
Short Row 3: Sl1 WYIF, P to 1 st before gap, P2tog, P1, turn.
Short Row 4: Sl1 WYIB, K to 1 st before gap, K2tog, K1, turn.
Rep Short Rows 3–4 another 4 (5) times. 19 (23) heel sts.

Gusset & Arch Shaping

Place held instep sts back on needle(s) if needed. Resume working in the rnd.

Setup Rnd: PM for BOR, PU and K 16 sts, work across instep sts in established ribbing pattern, PU and K 16 sts, PM, K to end. 80 (90) sts total; 61 (67) sts before M, 19 (23) sts after M.

Next Rnd: Work Gusset & Arch Pattern from chart or written instructions to M, SM, K to end.

Rep last rnd until Rnds 1–20 (1–18) of Gusset & Arch Pattern have been completed. 60 (72) sts total; 41 (49) sts before M, 19 (23) sts after M.

Next Rnd: Work subsequent rnd in Gusset & Arch Pattern Pattern to M, SM, K2, M1R, K to last 2 sts, M1L, K2.

Next Rnd: Work next rnd in Gusset & Arch Pattern to M, SM, K to end.

Rep last two rnds until Rnds 21–30 (19–30) of Gusset & Arch Pattern have been completed. 60 (72) sts total; 31 (37) sts for instep, 29 (35) sts for sole.

Foot

Next Rnd: Work Instep Pattern from chart or written instructions to M, K to end.

Cont as established, working subsequent rnds of Instep Pattern until foot length measures approx 1.75 (2)″ shorter than desired finished length, preferably ending with Rnd 5 of pattern.

Toe

Rnd 1: K1, SSK, work in established rib pattern to 3 sts before M, K2tog, K1, SM, K to end. 58 (70) sts.

Rnd 2: K2, work in established rib pattern to 2 sts before M, K2, SM, K to end.

Rnd 3: K1, SSK, work in established rib pattern to 3 sts before M, K2tog, K1, SM, K1, SSK, K to last 3 sts, K2tog, K1. 4 sts dec.

Rep Rnds 2–3 another 5 (7) times. 34 (38) sts.

Rep Rnd 3 four more times. 18 (22) sts.

Graft instep to sole sts using Kitchener Stitch.

Second Sock

Make second sock same as first.

Finishing

Weave in ends, wash, and block as desired.

Leg Pattern

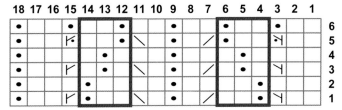

work rep sts 3 (4) times

Heel Flap Pattern

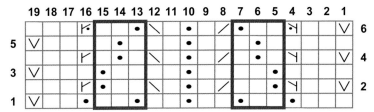

work rep sts 3 (4) times

LEGEND

	No Stitch Placeholder—no stitch made		**SSK** Slip, slip, knit slipped stitches together
	K RS: Knit stitch WS: Purl stitch		**M1R** Make 1 right-leaning stitch
•	**P** RS: Purl stitch WS: Knit stitch		**M1L** Make 1 left-leaning stitch
V	**Sl** RS: Slip stitch purl-wise, with yarn in back WS: Slip stitch purl-wise, with yarn in front		**M1PR** Make 1 right-leaning purl stitch
	K2tog Knit 2 stitches together as one stitch		**M1PL** Make 1 left-leaning purl stitch
			Pattern Repeat

Gusset & Arch Pattern

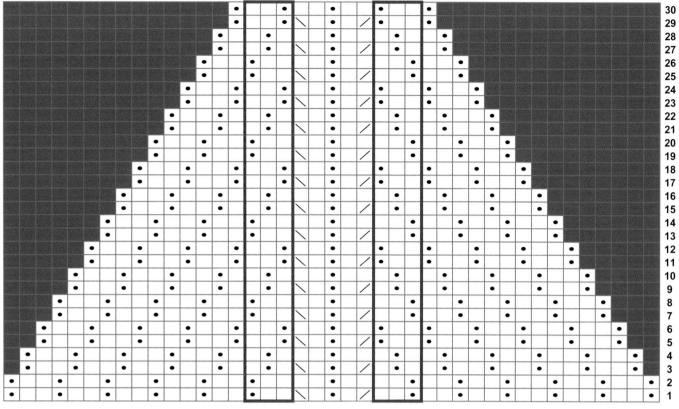

work rep sts 4 (5) times

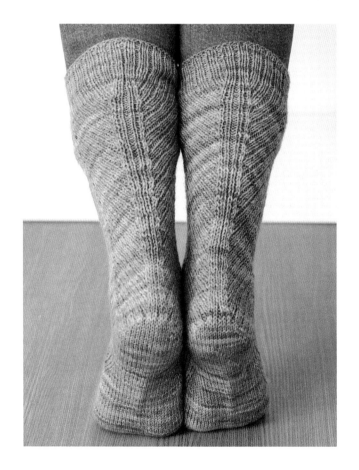

Instep Chart

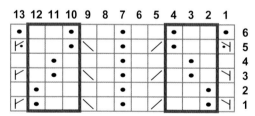

work rep sts 4 (5) times

DASHING
by Sarah Dobbins

FINISHED MEASUREMENTS

5.75 (6.5, 7.5, 8.5)" finished leg circumference, 5.75 (6.75, 7.75, 8.75)" finished foot circumference; meant to be worn with 5–10% negative ease (adjustable length)

YARN

Hawthorne™ (fingering weight, 80% Fine Superwash Highland Wool, 20% Polyamide (Nylon); 357 yards/100g): Jade District 27843, 1 hank

NEEDLES

US 1 (2.25mm) 32" circular needles for Magic Loop technique or DPNs, or size to obtain gauge

NOTIONS

Yarn Needle
Stitch Markers

GAUGE

32 sts and 46 rnds = 4" in Stockinette Stitch, blocked
34 sts and 46 rnds = 4" in Dash Stitch Pattern, blocked

For pattern support, contact sarah71208@gmail.com

Dashing

Notes:

A texture that is both pleasing to the eye and fun to knit, the dashed texture highlights the beautiful colors in variegated yarn.

Dashing Socks are knit top down using a "dashed" texture alternated with rows of stockinette. A faux heel flap and gusset is created using increases, a slip-stitch texture for the back of the heel, and short rows with decreases to create a square heel turn. The sock is finished with a rounded toe.

If knitting a sock longer than the largest circumference with foot length for a women's US 9/10 with a leg length of 4", a second skein may be needed.

As you make the first sock, it may be helpful to record the number of rounds worked for the leg and foot as a reference for the second sock.

Dash Stitch Pattern (DSP) (in the round over an even number of sts)
Rnds 1–2: K all.
Rnd 3: (YO, K2, pass YO over the 2 just-worked K sts) to end.
Rep Rnds 1–3 for pattern.

DIRECTIONS

Cuff
Using German Twisted Cast On, CO 48 (56, 64, 72) sts.
PM for BOR and join to work in the rnd, being careful not to twist sts.
Rnd 1: (K1 TBL, P1) to end.
Rep Rnd 1 until cuff is approx 1–1.5" long.

Leg
Work DSP until desired leg length is achieved, ending after Rnd 3. It is recommended that length of leg and cuff together is at least half the length of total foot length.

Heel & Gusset
Setup Rnd 1: K24 (28, 32, 36), PM, K24 (28, 32, 36).
First half of sock sts will be bottom of foot; second half of sts will be top of foot and will always be worked in DSP to end of rnd.
Setup Rnd 2: M1R, PM, (K1, Sl1) 12 (14, 16, 18) times, PM, M1L, SM, work DSP to end. 2 sts inc.
See diagram to view this division of sts:

Rnd 1: (K to M, SM) three times, work DSP to end.
Rnd 2: K to M, M1R, SM, (K1, Sl1) 12 (14, 16, 18) times, SM, M1L, K to M, SM, work DSP to end. 2 sts inc.
Rep Rnds 1–2 another 10 (12, 14, 16) times. 24 (28, 32, 36) gusset sts total.
Next Rnd: (K to M, remove M) two times, K to M, SM, work DSP to end.

Heel Turn
Heel turn is worked flat over heel sts only.
Short Row 1 (RS): K21 (24, 28, 31), PM, K6 (8, 8, 10), PM, SSK, turn.
Short Row 2 (WS): Sl1 WYIF, SM, P to M, SM, P2tog, turn.
Short Row 3: Sl1 WYIB, SM, K to M, SM, SSK, turn.
Short Row 4: Rep Row 2.
Rep Short Rows 3–4 another 9 (11, 13, 15) times.

Foot
Begin working in the rnd again.
Rnd 1: Sl1, SM, K to M, remove M, SSK, do not turn, K to next M, SM, work DSP to next M (old BOR M), SM, K to 2 sts before M, K2tog, remove M, K to M (this is new BOR). All Ms for heel turn have been removed. 48 (56, 64, 72) total sts.
Rnd 2: Work DSP to M, SM, K to end.
Rep Rnd 2 until foot is approx 1 (1.25, 1.5, 1.5)" shorter than desired sock length, ending with a K rnd.

Toe
For Sizes 5.75 (6.5, -, -)" start on Rnd 5; for Sizes - (-, 7.5, 8.5)" start on Rnd 1.
Rnd 1: (K1, SSK, K to 3 sts before M, K2tog, K1, SM) two times. 4 sts dec.
Rnds 2–4: K all.
Rnd 5: Rep Rnd 1.
Rnds 6–7: K all.
Rnd 8: Rep Rnd 1.
Rnd 9: K all.
Rep Rnd 1 until 12 (16, 20, 24) sts remain.

Finishing
Remove Ms and graft toe closed using Kitchener Stitch. Weave in ends, wash, and block as desired.

Second Sock
Make second sock same as first.

faux heel flap

gusset inc (after M)   gusset inc (before M)

DELICATE
by Aimee Sher

FINISHED MEASUREMENTS

7 (8, 9)" circumference × adjustable foot length; meant to be worn with approx 10% negative ease

YARN

Hawthorne™ (fingering weight, 80% Fine Superwash Highland Wool, 20% Polyamide (Nylon); 357 yards/100g): Sweet Home Tonal 27409, 1 hank

NEEDLES

US 1.5 (2.5mm) 24" circular needles

US 1.5 (2.5mm) DPNs or two circular needles for two circulars technique or 32" or longer circular needles for Magic Loop technique, or size to obtain gauge (note that if using a 9" circular, one of the other needles listed will be needed for heel and toe)

NOTIONS

Yarn Needle
Stitch Markers
Locking Stitch Markers

GAUGE

32 sts and 34 rnds = 4" in Stockinette Stitch in the round, blocked

For pattern support, contact aimeeshermakes@gmail.com

Delicate

Notes:

Inspired by the beautiful colors of Hawthorne Hand Painted yarns, this pattern features gentle waves of lace and ruffles that combine and echo each other and mimic the gentle color changes of the yarn.

Delicate Socks are anklet socks, knit top down in one continuous construction method, with fold-over ruffled cuffs and lace panels. The folded cuff includes a hidden rib panel for a close fit under the stockinette outer layer. Delicate is engaging to knit and features interesting techniques that are a total breeze to work.

Chart is worked in the round; read each chart row from right to left as a RS row.

Lace Chart (in the round over 17 sts)

Rnd 1: SSK three times, (YO, K1) five times, YO, K2tog three times.
Rnds 2-4: K all.
Rnds 5-6: Rep Rnds 1-2.
Rnd 7: P3, K3, P5, K3, P3.
Rnd 8: K all.
Rnds 9-12: Rep Rnds 7-8 two times.
Rep Rnds 1-12 for pattern.

Make DS (Make Double Stitch)

Sl1 P-wise with yarn in front. Bring yarn up, over, and back to pull on the slipped st until it slides around to show two legs. It will look like a double st, but count this as a single st. Work following sts as usual while keeping tension on slipped st.
K DS= K through both legs (through center of entire bundle) as if DS were a normal single st. Work following sts as usual.

DIRECTIONS

Ruffle Cast On

Using the 24" needle and Long Tail Cast On, CO 168 (192, 216) sts. Join to work in the rnd, being careful not to twist sts; PM for BOR.
Knit ten rnds.
Switch to needles for small circumference knitting for the following Rnd.
Rnd 11: (K3tog) around to end. 56 (64, 72) sts.

Outer Cuff

Knit 25 rnds. Pay special attention to tension for first few rnds, keeping tension taut to ensure the ruffle does not stretch these rnds to a different gauge.
Rnd 26: K all; turn.
Rnd 27: Make DS, turn work inside out; P1, (K1, P1) to BOR. Work in this direction for remainder of pattern. The previous WS is now the RS. The section worked before this will be folded over the inner cuff.

Inner Cuff

Rnd 1: K DS, P1, (K1, P1) to end.
Work 1x1 Rib as established for 23 more rnds.

Heel Flap

Setup Row: Remove BOR M, K28 (32, 36), place those sts on hold, K to end, turn. Heel flap is worked back and forth across these 28 (32, 36) sts.
3 edge sts on heel flap are worked in Garter Stitch, while rest of heel flap is St st, worked as follows.

Row 1 (WS): K3, P to last 3 sts, K3.
Row 2 (RS): K across.
Rep Rows 1-2 another 13 (14, 15) times, then Rep Row 1 once more. There will be 15 (16, 17) garter bumps along each side of the heel flap.

Heel Turn

Short Row 1 (RS): Sl1 WYIB, K15 (17, 19), SSK, K1, turn.
Short Row 2 (WS): Sl1 WYIF, P5, P2tog, P1, turn.
Short Row 3 (RS): Sl1 WYIB, K to 1 st before gap, SSK, K1, turn.
Short Row 4 (WS): Sl1 WYIF, P to 1 st before gap, P2tog, P1, turn.
Rep Short Rows 3-4 until all heel sts have been worked. On final rep there might be no sts after the SSK and P2tog to work before turn—skip that st and turn. 16 (18, 20) sts remain on heel.
End Heel Row (RS): Knit across heel sts and turn work clockwise 90 degrees for gusset pick up.

Gusset

Because st pattern on foot has an odd number, gusset pick up and lace setup are worked at the same time, differently for each sock, working in the rnd again as follows.

First Sock Only
Setup Rnd: PU and K 15 (16, 17) sts, 1 before each purl bump along garter edge; PM for side, K6 (8, 10), PM, K17, PM, K5 (7, 9), PM for side; PU and K 15 (16, 17), 1 after each purl bump along second garter edge, K8 (9, 10) heel sts; PM (unique M) for BOR.

Second Sock Only
Setup Rnd: PU and K 15 (16, 17) sts, 1 before each purl bump along garter edge; PM for side, K5 (7, 9), PM, K17, PM, K6 (8, 10), PM for side; PU and K 15 (16, 17), 1 after each purl bump along second garter edge, K8 (9, 10) heel sts; PM (unique M) for BOR.

Resume both socks. 74 (82, 90) sts.

Gusset & Foot

Rnd 1: K to 3 sts before side M, K2tog, K1, SM, K to M, SM, work Lace Chart from chart or written instructions to M, SM, K to M, SM, K1, SSK, K to end. 2 sts dec.
Rnd 2: (K to M, SM) two times, work Lace Chart to M, SM, K to M, SM, K to end.
Rep Rnds 1-2 eight more times, working Lace Chart as established. 56 (64, 72) sts remain.

Cont working in the rnd, keeping top of foot in Lace Chart as established and knitting all other sts, until piece is 2.25 (2.5, 2.75)" shorter than desired length.

Stop working Lace Chart for toe section. Remove lace Ms.

Toe

Rnd 1: K all.
Rnd 2: (K1, SSK, K to 3 sts before M, K2tog, K1, SM) two times. 4 sts dec.
Rep Rnds 1–2 another 8 (10, 11) times. 20 (20, 24) sts remain.

Break yarn, leaving a long tail for grafting. Graft remaining sts closed with equal number of sts on two needles, using Kitchener Stitch.

Second Sock

Make second sock as first, paying special attention to setup in Gusset section, which differs from first sock.

Finishing

Weave in ends, wash, and block as desired.

LEGEND

 Knit Stitch

⊡ Purl Stitch

◉ **YO**
Yarn over

◢ **K2tog**
Knit 2 stitches together as one stitch

◣ **SSK**
Slip, slip, knit slipped stitches together

Delicate Chart

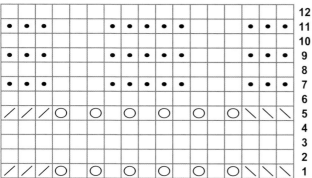

17	16	15	14	13	12	11	10	9	8	7	6	5	4	3	2	1	
																	12
•	•	•				•	•	•	•	•				•	•	•	11
																	10
•	•	•				•	•	•	•	•				•	•	•	9
																	8
•	•	•				•	•	•	•	•				•	•	•	7
																	6
/	/	/	O		O		O		O		O		O	\	\	\	5
																	4
																	3
																	2
/	/	/	O		O		O		O		O		O	\	\	\	1

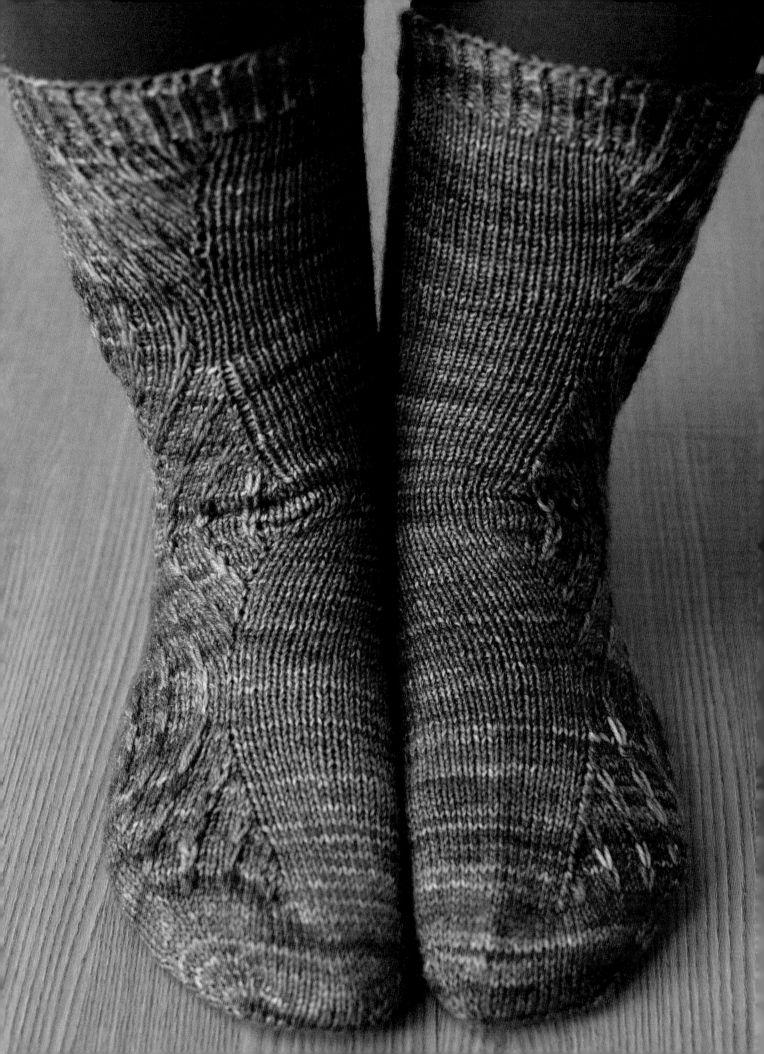

EMERGENT PROPERTIES
by Carolyn Lisle

FINISHED MEASUREMENTS
6.5 (7.25, 8.25)" foot circumference ×
8.25 (9, 9.75)" foot length, to fit US shoe
sizes 5–6.5 (7–8.5, 9–10.5); meant to be
worn with approx 10% negative ease;
foot length is adjustable

YARN
Muse™ Hand Painted Sock Yarn
(fingering weight, 75% Superwash
Merino Wool, 25% Nylon; 423
yards/100g): Elation 28153, 1 hank

NEEDLES
US 1 (2.25mm) DPNs or 32" or longer
circular needles for Magic Loop
technique, or size to obtain gauge

US 0 (2.0mm) DPNs or 32" or longer
circular needles for Magic Loop
technique, or one size smaller than
size used to obtain gauge

NOTIONS
Yarn Needle
Stitch Markers (5)
Sock Blockers

GAUGE
35 sts and 46 rnds = 4" in Stockinette
Stitch in the round, blocked (stitch
pattern gauges are consistent with
Stockinette Stitch gauge)

For pattern support, contact patternsupport@periwinkledragon.ca

Emergent Properties

Notes:

Like a flock of birds collectively swooping through the air due to the small movements of each individual, the large, bold motif on these socks emerges beautifully from a series of smaller repeating sequences.

Emergent Properties Socks feature a front panel of bias-shifted slipped stitches that is mirrored on the left and right socks, as well as a complementary motif on the back of the leg. They are constructed toe-up with a gusset, a reinforced heel flap, and a twisted-rib cuff. German short rows are used for the heel turn.

Always slip stitches purl-wise with yarn held to wrong side unless specified otherwise.

Charts are worked in the round; read each chart row from right to left as a RS row.

K1E2 (Knit 1 Elongated Twice)

Wrap yarn around RH needle three times while working a K st. The two extra wraps will unravel to make one long st when the st is slipped on the next rnd.

make DS (make Double Stitch)

Sl1 P-wise WYIF, then bring yarn over RH needle from front to back, pulling slipped st up and over so it looks like a double st. (See German Short Rows technique in Glossary.)

Emergent Properties Chart (in the round over 14 sts)

Left Sock begins pattern at Rnd 1; Right Sock begins pattern at Rnd 37.

Rnd 1: K2, (K1E2, K3) three times.
Rnd 2: M1R, K2, (Sl1, K3) two times, Sl1, K1, SSK.
Rnd 3: (K3, Sl1) three times, K2.
Rnd 4: M1R, (K3, Sl1) three times, SSK.
Rnd 5: (K1E2, K3) two times, K1E2, K5.
Rnd 6: M1R, (Sl1, K3) three times, SSK.
Rnd 7: K1, (Sl1, K3) two times, Sl1, K4.
Rnd 8: M1R, K1, (Sl1, K3) two times, Sl1, K2, SSK.
Rnds 9–24: Rep Rnds 1–8 two more times.
Rnds 25–26: Rep Rnds 1–2.
Rnds 27–28: Rep Rnd 3.
Rnd 29: (K3, K1E2) three times, K2.
Rnd 30: Rep Rnd 3.
Rnds 31–34: Rep Rnds 27–30.
Rnds 35–36: Rep Rnd 3.
Rnd 37: Rep Rnd 29.
Rnd 38: K2tog, K1, (Sl1, K3) two times, Sl1, K2, M1L.
Rnd 39: K2, (Sl1, K3) three times.
Rnd 40: K2tog, (Sl1, K3) three times, M1L.
Rnd 41: K5, (K1E2, K3) two times, K1E2.
Rnd 42: K2tog, (K3, Sl1) three times, M1L.
Rnd 43: K4, (Sl1, K3) two times, Sl1, K1.
Rnd 44: K2tog, K2, (Sl1, K3) two times, Sl1, K1, M1L.
Rnds 45–60: Rep Rnds 37–44 two more times.
Rnds 61–62: Rep Rnds 37–38.
Rnds 63–64: Rep Rnd 39.

Rnd 65: Rep Rnd 1.
Rnd 66: Rep Rnd 39.
Rnds 67–70: Rep Rnds 63–66.
Rnds 71–72: Rep Rnd 39.
Rep Rnds 1–72 for pattern.

Emergent Leg Chart (in the round over 7 sts)

Rnd 1: K3, K1E2, K3.
Rnd 2: K3, Sl1, K3.
Rnd 3: K1E2, K2, Sl1, K2, K1E2.
Rnd 4: Sl1, K2, Sl1, K2, Sl1.
Rnd 5: Sl1, K2, K1E2, K2, Sl1.
Rnd 6: Rep Rnd 4.
Rep Rnds 3–6 for pattern.
Rnds 7–8: Rep Rnd 2.

1x1 Twisted Rib (in the round over an even number of sts)

Rnd 1: (K1 TBL, P1) to end.
Rep Rnd 1 for pattern.

DIRECTIONS

Left Sock

Toe

CO 24 sts on larger needles using Judy's Magic Cast On. PM for BOR.
Setup Rnd: K all.
Rnd 1: (K1, YO, K10, YO, K1) two times. 28 sts.
Rnd 2: (K1, K1 TBL, K1, YO, K8, YO, K1, K1 TBL, K1) two times. 32 sts.
Rnd 3: (K1, YO, K2, K1 TBL, K8, K1 TBL, K2, YO, K1) two times. 36 sts.
Rnd 4: (K1, K1 TBL, K1, YO, K12, YO, K1, K1 TBL, K1) two times. 40 sts.
Rnd 5: (K3, K1 TBL, K12, K1 TBL, K3) two times.
Rnd 6: (K1, YO, K18, YO, K1) two times. 44 sts.
Rnd 7: (K1, K1 TBL, K1, YO, K16, YO, K1, K1 TBL, K1) two times. 48 sts.
Rnd 8: (K3, K1 TBL, K16, K1 TBL, K3) two times.
Rnd 9: (K1, YO, K22, YO, K1) two times. 52 sts.
Rnd 10: (K1, K1 TBL, K1, YO, K20, YO, K1, K1 TBL, K1) two times. 56 sts.
Rnd 11: (K3, K1 TBL, K20, K1 TBL, K3) two times.

Sizes - (7.25, 8.25)" Only

Rnd 12: (K1, YO, K26, YO, K1) two times. 60 sts.
Rnd 13: (K1, K1 TBL, K1, YO, K24, YO, K1, K1 TBL, K1) two times. 64 sts.
Rnd 14: (K3, K1 TBL, K24, K1 TBL, K3) two times.

Size 8.25" Only

Rnd 15: (K1, YO, K30, YO, K1) two times. 68 sts.
Rnd 16: (K1, K1 TBL, K1, YO, K28, YO, K1, K1 TBL, K1) two times. 72 sts.
Rnd 17: (K3, K1 TBL, K28, K1 TBL, K3) two times.

Foot (resume all sizes)
Setup Rnd 1: K28 (32, 36), PM, K to end. 56 (64, 72) sts.
Setup Rnd 2: K to M, SM, K0 (1, 2), work Emergent Properties Chart Rnd 1 from chart or written instructions, K to end.
Rnd 1: K to M, SM, K0 (1, 2), work next Emergent Properties Chart rnd, K to end.
Rep Rnd 1 until Emergent Properties Chart Rnd 44 is complete for stated foot lengths, or until foot length is 3.25 (3.75, 4.25)" shorter than desired length (ending after an Emergent Properties Chart rnd divisible by 4).

Gusset Shaping
Rnd 2: K to M, SM, M1R, PM, K0 (1, 2), work next Emergent Properties Chart rnd, K to end, PM, M1L. 2 sts inc.
Rnd 3: K to second M, SM, K0 (1, 2), work next Emergent Properties Chart rnd, K to end.
Rnd 4: K to second M, M1R, SM, K0 (1, 2), work next Emergent Properties Chart rnd, K to third M, SM, M1L, K to end. 2 sts inc.
Rep Rnds 3–4 another 12 (14, 16) times. 14 (16, 18) sts in each gusset; 84 (96, 108) sts total.
Rep Rnd 3 once more.

Heel Turn
The heel is worked flat on sole sts only.
Short Row 1 (RS): K14 (16, 18), M1L, K to 1 st before first M, turn, make DS. 29 (33, 37) sole sts; 85 (97, 109) sts total.
Short Row 2 (WS): P to 1 st before BOR, turn, make DS.
Short Row 3: K to 1 st before DS, turn, make DS.
Short Row 4: P to 1 st before DS, turn, make DS.
Rep Short Rows 3–4 another 3 (4, 5) times. 9 center sts between last two DSs.
Next Short Row (RS): K to first M, remove M, turn.
Next Short Row (WS): Sl1 WYIF, P to BOR. Remove BOR M and turn.

Heel Flap
Short Row 1 (RS): Sl1 K-wise WYIB, K1, (Sl1, K1) 13 (15, 17) times, SSK, turn. 1 st dec from gusset.
Short Row 2 (WS): Sl1 P-wise WYIF, P27 (31, 35), P2tog, turn. 1 st dec.
Short Row 3: Sl1 K-wise WYIB, K2, (Sl1, K1) 12 (14, 16) times, K1, SSK, turn. 1 st dec.
Short Row 4: Rep Short Row 2.
Rep Short Rows 1–4 another 6 (7, 8) times. No gusset sts remain; 57 (65, 73) sts total.

Leg
Setup Rnd: Sl1 K-wise, K10 (12, 14), PM, work Emergent Leg Chart Rnd 1, K to next M, remove M, PU and K TBL 1 st across the gap, PM, K0 (1, 2), work next Emergent Properties Chart rnd (as established from foot), K to next M, remove M, PU and K TBL 1 st across the gap, PM for BOR. 59 (67, 75) sts.
Rnd 1: K to first M, SM, work next Emergent Leg Chart rnd, K to second M, SM, K0 (1, 2), work next Emergent Properties Chart rnd, K to end.
Rep Rnd 1 until Emergent Properties Chart Rnd 60 is complete. The last Emergent Leg Chart rnd worked is Rnd 4.

Rep Rnd 1 four more times to work Emergent Leg Chart Rnds 5–8 and Emergent Properties Chart Rnds 61–64.

Cuff
Change to smaller needles.

Sizes 6.5 (-, 8.25)" Only
Setup Rnd 1: K all, removing all Ms except BOR M.
Setup Rnd 2: (K1 TBL, P1) to last 3 sts, K1 TBL, P2tog. 58 (-, 74) sts.

Size 7.25" Only
Setup Rnd 1: K all, removing first M only.
Setup Rnd 2: (K1 TBL, P1) to 1 st before M, K2tog TBL and remove M, P1, (K1 TBL, P1) to end. 66 sts.

Resume All Sizes
Work 1x1 Twisted Rib for eleven rnds.
BO using Jeny's Surprisingly Stretchy Bind Off.

Right Sock
Toe
Rep Left Sock toe instructions.

Foot
Setup Rnd 1: K42 (48, 54), PM, K to end. 56 (64, 72) sts.
Setup Rnd 2: K to M, SM, K0 (1, 2), work Emergent Properties Chart Rnd 37 from chart or written instructions, K to end.
Rnd 1: K to M, SM, K0 (1, 2), work next Emergent Properties Chart rnd, K to end.
Rep Rnd 1 until Emergent Properties Chart Rnd 8 is complete for stated foot lengths, or until foot length is 3.25 (3.75, 4.25)" shorter than desired length (ending after an Emergent Properties Chart rnd divisible by 4).

Gusset Shaping
Rnd 2: K28 (32, 36), PM, M1R, PM, K to M, SM, K0 (1, 2), work next Emergent Properties Chart rnd, K0 (1, 2) to end, PM, M1L. 2 sts inc.
Rnd 3: K to third M, SM, K0 (1, 2), work next Emergent Properties Chart rnd, K to end.
Rnd 4: K to second M, M1R, SM, K to third M, SM, K0 (1, 2), work next Emergent Properties Chart rnd, K0 (1, 2) to fourth M, SM, M1L, K to end. 2 sts inc.
Rep Rnds 3–4 another 12 (14, 16) times. 14 (16, 18) sts in each gusset; 84 (96, 108) sts total.
Rep Rnd 3 once more.

Heel
Rep Left Sock Heel Turn and Heel Flap instructions.

Leg
Setup Rnd: Sl1 K-wise, K10 (12, 14), PM, work Emergent Leg Chart Rnd 1, K to next M, remove M, PU and K TBL 1 st across the gap, K to next M, SM, K0 (1, 2), work next Emergent Properties Chart rnd (as established from foot), K0 (1, 2) to next M, remove M, PU and K TBL 1 st across the gap, PM for BOR. 59 (67, 75) sts.

Rnd 1: K to first M, SM, work next Emergent Leg Chart rnd, K to second M, SM, K0 (1, 2), work next Emergent Properties Chart rnd, K to end.

Rep Rnd 1 until Emergent Properties Chart Rnd 24 is complete. The last Emergent Leg Chart rnd worked is Rnd 4. Rep Rnd 1 four more times to work Emergent Leg Chart Rnds 5–8 and Emergent Properties Chart Rnds 25–28.

Cuff

Change to smaller needles.

Sizes 6.5 (-, 8.25)" Only

Setup Rnd 1: K all, removing first and third Ms only.
Setup Rnd 2: (K1 TBL, P1) to 1 st before M, K2tog TBL and remove M, P1, (K1 TBL, P1) to end. 58 (-, 74) sts.

Size 7.25" Only

Setup Rnd 1: K all, removing all Ms except BOR M.
Setup Rnd 2: (K1 TBL, P1) to last 3 sts, K1 TBL, P2tog. 66 sts.

Resume All Sizes

Work 1x1 Twisted Rib for eleven rnds.
BO using Jeny's Surprisingly Stretchy Bind Off.

Finishing

Weave in ends, wash, and block as desired.

Emergent Properties Chart

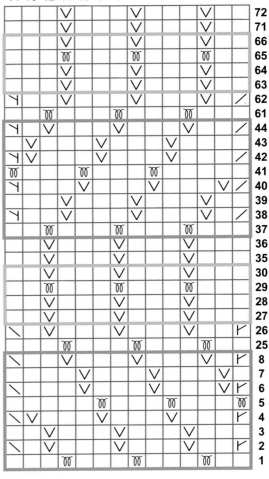

Leg Chart

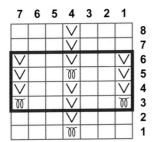

LEGEND

☐ **Knit Stitch**

Ⅴ **Sl**
Slip stitch purl-wise, with yarn in back

⬚ **K1E2 (knit 1 elongated twice)**
Knit 1 stitch wrapping yarn three times; drop extra wraps from needle on next row

⼁ **M1R**
Make 1 right-leaning stitch

⼁ **M1L**
Make 1 left-leaning stitch

◿ **K2tog**
Knit 2 stitches together as one stitch

◺ **SSK**
Slip, slip, knit slipped stitches together

☐ **Pattern Repeat**

☐ **Work Rnds Two Times**

☐ **Work Rnds Three Times**

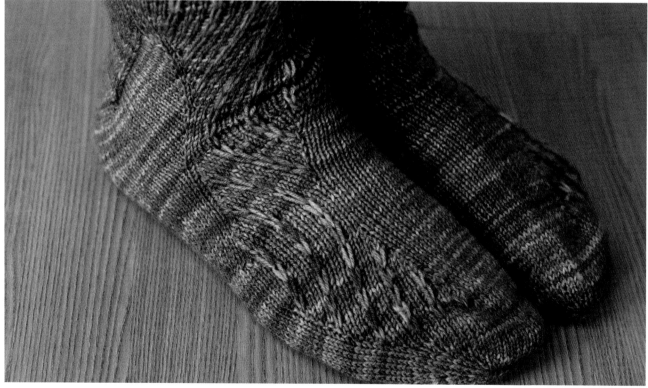

EXTRA FROSTING
by Brenda K.B. Anderson

FINISHED MEASUREMENTS

6.25 (7, 7.75, 8.75)" foot circumference × 7.75 (8.75, 9.5, 10)" foot length, to fit US shoe sizes 4–6.5 (7–9.5, 10–12, 12.5–14.5); meant to be worn with approx 10% negative ease (easily customizable)

YARN

Static™ (fingering weight, 75% Superwash Wool, 25% Nylon; 437 yards/100g): Paradise 28495, 1 (1, 2, 2) hanks

NEEDLES

US 0 (2.0mm) DPNs or two circular needles for two circulars technique or 32" or longer circular needles for Magic Loop technique, or size to obtain gauge

NOTIONS

Yarn Needle
Stitch Markers

GAUGE

35 sts and 48 rnds = 4" in Stockinette Stitch in the round, blocked
41 sts and 48 rnds = 4" in 2x6 Rib in the round, blocked (note that this is approximate due to the amount of stretch in the ribbing)
46 sts and 48 rnds = 4" in 1x1 Rib in the round, blocked (note that this is approximate due to the amount of stretch in the ribbing)

For pattern support, contact yarnville@gmail.com

Extra Frosting

Notes:

Inspired by layers of extra frosting that decorate a birthday cake, these fun socks feature perfectly ruched ankles, thanks to several columns of slip stitches. The fun details in this design are highlighted by this visually complex yarn.

These top-down socks begin with a German Twisted Cast On followed by 1x1 Rib for the cuff. The super-easy ruched pattern for the ankle is next, followed by the slip stitch heel flap, turned heel and gusset. The columns of slip stitches morph into knit-2 ridges against the purled background on the top of the instep. The heel, sole and toe of sock are all smooth Stockinette Stitch.

Sizing/Fit

Choose a size with 0.75–1″ of negative ease in foot circumference. Knit the foot length of sock to approx 0.75–1″ shorter than actual foot measurement. Foot length is easy to customize. Yardage depends on both foot circumference and length. If you knit length of foot to a longer or shorter length this will affect required yarn amounts.

Always slip stitches purl-wise with yarn held to wrong side unless specified otherwise.

DIRECTIONS

Ribbed Cuff

Using German Twisted Cast On method (or other stretchy cast on), CO 72 (80, 88, 96) sts. Being careful not to twist, join to work in the rnd.
Work 1x1 Rib for 14 (16, 18, 20) rnds.

Leg

Rnd 1: (P6, K2) to end.
Rnds 2–6: (P6, Sl2) to end.
Rep Rows 1–6 another 12 (13, 14, 16) times.
Rep Rnd 1 once more.
Next Rnd (partial rnd): (P6, K2) three times (leave remaining sts un-worked) to reposition BOR.

Heel Flap

Turn work. The next 42 (42, 50, 50) sts will be worked back and forth for heel flap.
Rnd 1 (WS): Sl1 P-wise WYIF, P41 (41, 49, 49), turn.
Rnd 2 (RS): Sl1 K-wise WYIB, (K1, Sl1 WYIB) to last st, K1, turn.
Rep Rows 1–2 another 11 (12, 13, 15) times.
Rep Row 1 once more.
There are a total of 25 (27, 29, 33) rows in heel flap; flap measures approx 1.75 (2, 2.25. 2.5)″ tall.

Heel Turn

Short Row 1 (RS): Sl1 K-wise WYIB, K22 (22, 28, 28), SSK, K1, turn. 1 st dec.
Short Row 2 (WS): Sl1 P-wise WYIF, P5, P2tog, P1, turn. 1 st dec.
Short Row 3: Sl1 K-wise WYIB, K until 1 st remains before gap, SSK, K1, turn. 1 st dec.
Short Row 4: Sl1 P-wise WYIF, P until 1 st remains before gap, P2tog, P1, turn. 1 st dec.
Rep Short Rows 3–4 until all heel sts have been worked. 24 (24, 28, 28) heel sts after working last WS row.
Final Heel Row: With RS facing, Sl1 K-wise WYIB, K23 (23, 27, 27).

Gusset

Setup Rnd: PU and K 14 (15, 16, 17) sts along side of heel flap, PM, (P6, K2) 3 (4, 4, 5) times, P6, PM, PU and K 14 (15, 16, 17) sts along other edge of heel flap, K12 (12, 14, 14) leaving last 12 (12, 14, 14) sts un-worked, PM for new BOR. Remove previous BOR M. 82 (92, 98, 108) sts.

Rnd 1: K to M, (P6, K2) 3 (4, 4, 5) times, P6, K to end.
Rnd 2: K to 2 sts before M, K2tog, SM, (P6, K2) 3 (4, 4, 5) times, P6, SM, SSK, K to end. 2 sts dec.
Rep Rnds 1–2 another 10 (11, 10, 11) times. 11 (12, 11, 12) dec rnds; 22 (24, 22, 24) sts dec; 60 (68, 76, 84) sts total.

Foot

Rnd 1: K to M, (P6, K2) 3 (4, 4, 5) times, P6, K to end.
Rep Rnd 1 until sock measures 6.25 (7.25, 8, 8.5)″ from back corner of heel or approx 1.25 (1.5, 1.75, 1.75)″ shorter than desired length.
Next Rnd: K all.

Toe

Setup Rnd: Remove BOR M, K15 (17, 19, 21), PM for new BOR; K30 (34, 38, 42), place contrasting M, K30 (34, 38, 42) ending at BOR M. Two new Ms placed, remove all other Ms.
Rnd 1: (K1, SSK, K to 3 sts before M, K2tog, K1, SM) two times. 4 sts dec.
Rnd 2: K all.
Rep Rnds 1–2 another 3 (4, 5, 6) times.
Rep Rnd 1 five more times. 24 (28, 32, 36) sts.
Break yarn, leaving long tail for sewing.
Use Kitchener Stitch to graft toe closed.

Second Sock

Make second sock same as first.

Finishing

Weave in all ends. Wash and block as desired.

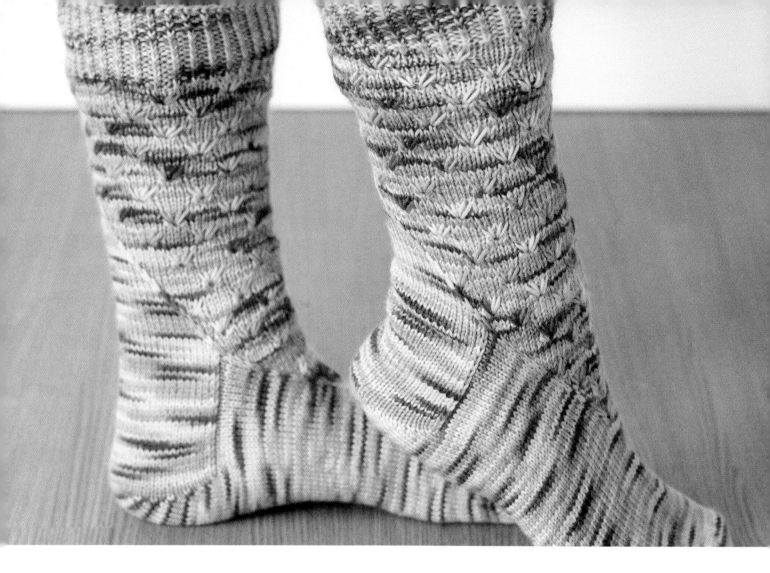

FLOWERING MEADOW
by Mone Dräger

FINISHED MEASUREMENTS

7 (8, 9)" leg circumference × 8 (9, 10)" foot length × 8 (9, 10) leg length, customizable; meant to be worn with approx 10% negative ease

YARN

Stroll™ Hand Painted (fingering weight, 75% Fine Superwash Merino Wool, 25% Nylon, 462 yards/100g): Frolic 28276, 1 hank

NEEDLES

US 1 (2.25mm) two 24" circular needles for two circulars technique or 32" or longer circular needles for Magic Loop technique, or size to obtain gauge (DPNs are not recommended due to construction)

NOTIONS

Yarn Needle
Stitch Markers
Cable Needle
Scrap Yarn or Stitch Holder (optional)

GAUGE

32 sts and 44 rnds = 4" in Stockinette Stitch in the round, blocked
32 sts and 44 rnds = 4" in Leg Pattern in the round, blocked

For pattern support, contact mone.draeger@web.de

Flowering Meadow

Notes:

Who doesn't enjoy the sight of a flower meadow, bursting with colors and forms? The stitch pattern used in these socks forms small motifs reminiscent of flowers, which emerge from a background of Stockinette Stitch.

The socks are knit toe-up with a gusset and heel flap. Gusset increases are worked as part of the instep pattern on the top of the foot. The foot length is customizable, but the Instep Pattern needs to be worked in full to get the correct stitch count; Instep Pattern and heel turn add approx 4 (4.75, 5.25)″ to the total length. The leg length can be altered by working fewer or more repeats of the Leg pattern.

Always slip stitches purl-wise with yarn held to wrong side.

Charts are worked in the rnd; read each chart row from right to left as a RS row.

Twisted Rib (in the round over an even number of sts)
Rnd 1: (K1 TBL, P1) to end.
Rep Rnd 1 for pattern.

LL (Left-leaning Loop)
Insert LH needle between first and second st on RH needle three rnds below, between the decs worked in that rnd; wrap yarn around needle and pull a long loop through (loop must be long enough to span comfortably across previous rnds); place loop on RH needle. 1 st inc.

RL (Right-leaning Loop)
Insert RH needle between first and second st on LH needle two rnds below, between the decs worked in that rnd; wrap yarn around needle and pull a long loop through, up on to needle (loop must be long enough to span comfortably across previous rnds). 1 st inc.

LT (Left Twist)
Sl1 to CN, hold in front, K1, K1 from CN.

RT (Right Twist)
Sl1 to CN, hold in back, K1, K1 from CN.

Instep Pattern (in the round beginning with 4 sts)
Rnd 1: K2tog, SSK. 2 sts.
Rnd 2: K all.
Rnd 3: RL, K2, LL. 4 sts.
Rnd 4: Sl1, K2, Sl1.
Rnd 5: K1, M1L, K2, M1R, K1. 6 sts.
Rnd 6: Sl1, K4, Sl1.
Rnd 7: K1, M1L, K4, M1R, K1. 8 sts.
Rnd 8: Sl1, K6, Sl1.
Rnd 9: K1, M1L, K1, K2tog, SSK, K1, M1R, K1.
Rnd 10: Rep Rnd 8.
Rnd 11: K1, M1L, K2, RL, K2, LL, K2, M1R, K1. 12 sts.
Rnd 12: Sl1, K10, Sl1.
Rnd 13: K1, M1L, K10, M1R, K1. 14 sts.
Rnd 14: Sl1, K2tog, SSK, K4, K2tog, SSK, Sl1. 10 sts.
Rnd 15: K1, M1L, K8, M1R, K1. 12 sts.

Rnd 16: Sl1, K1, RL, K2, LL, K4, RL, K2, LL, K1, Sl1. 16 sts.
Rnd 17: K1, M1L, K14, M1R, K1. 18 sts.
Rnd 18: Sl1, K16, Sl1.
Rnd 19: K1, M1L, (SSK, K4, K2tog) two times, M1R, K1. 16 sts.
Rnd 20: Sl1, K14, Sl1.
Rnd 21: K1, M1L, (K2, LL, K4, RL) two times, K2, M1R, K1. 22 sts.
Rnd 22: Sl1, K20, Sl1.
Rnd 23: K1, M1L, K20, M1R, K1. 24 sts.
Rnd 24: Sl1, K5, K2tog, SSK, K4, K2tog, SSK, K5, Sl1. 20 sts.
Rnd 25: K1, M1L, K18, M1R, K1. 22 sts.
Rnd 26: Sl1, K6, RL, K2, LL, K4, RL, K2, LL, K6, Sl1. 26 sts.
Rnd 27: K1, M1L, K24, M1R, K1. 28 sts.
Rnd 28: Sl1, K26, Sl1.
Rnd 29: K1, M1L, K3, (K2tog, SSK, K4) two times, K2tog, SSK, K3, M1R, K1. 24 sts.
Rnd 30: Sl1, K22, Sl1.
Rnd 31: K1, M1L, (K4, RL, K2, LL) three times, K4, M1R, K1. 32 sts.
Rnd 32: Sl1, K30, Sl1.
Rnd 33: K1, M1L, K30, M1R, K1. 34 sts.
Rnd 34: Sl1, K2, (K2tog, SSK, K4) three times, K2tog, SSK, K2, Sl1. 26 sts.
Rnd 35: Rep Rnd 27. 28 sts.

Leg Traverse Pattern (in the round over varying st counts)
Start on Rnd 1 (5, 9).
Rnd 1: K14, Sl1, K26, Sl1, K14. 56 sts.
Rnd 2: K13, RT, K3, (K2tog, SSK, K4) two times, K2tog, SSK, K3, LT, K13. 50 sts.
Rnd 3: K13, Sl1, K22, Sl1, K13.
Rnd 4: K13, M1L, (K4, RL, K2, LL) three times, K4, LT, K12. 56 sts.
Rnd 5: K12 (16, -), Sl1, K30, Sl1, K12 (16, -). 56 (64, -) sts.
Rnd 6: K11 (15, -), RT, K30, LT, K11 (15, -).
Rnd 7: K11 (15, -), Sl1, K2, (K2tog, SSK, K4) three times, K2tog, SSK, K2, Sl1, K11 (15, -). 48 (56, -) sts.
Rnd 8: K10 (14, -), RT, K24, LT, K10 (14, -).
Rnd 9: K10 (14, 18), Sl1, K3, (RL, K2, LL, K4) three times, RL, K2, LL, K3, Sl1, K10 (14, 18). 56 (64, 72) sts.
Rnd 10: K9 (13, 17), RT, K34, LT, K9 (13, 17).
Rnd 11: K9 (13, 17), Sl1, K36, Sl1, K9 (13, 17).
Rnd 12: K8 (12, 16), RT, (K2tog, SSK, K4) four times, K2tog, SSK, LT, K8 (12, 16). 46 (54, 62) sts.
Rnd 13: K8 (12, 16) Sl1, K28, Sl1, K8 (12, 16).
Rnd 14: K7 (11, 15), RT, K1, (RL, K2, LL, K4) four times, RL, K2, LL, K1, LT, K7 (11, 15). 56 (64, 72) sts.
Rnd 15: K7 (11) 15, Sl1, K40, Sl1, K7 (11, 15).
Rnd 16: K6 (10, 14), RT, K40, LT, K6 (10, 14).
Rnd 17: K14, Sl1, K1, (SSK, K4, K2tog) five times, K1, Sl1, K14. 46 (54, 62) sts.
Rnd 18: K5 (9, 13), RT, K32, LT, K5 (9, 13).
Rnd 19: K5 (9, 13), Sl1, K3, (LL, K4, RL, K2) four times, LL, K4, RL, K3, Sl1, K5 (9, 13). 56 (64, 72) sts.
Rnd 20: K4 (8, 12), RT, K44, LT, K4 (8, 12).
Rnd 21: K4 (8, 12), Sl1, K46, Sl1, K4 (8, 12).

Rnd 22: K3 (7, 11), RT, K5, (K2tog, SSK, K4) four times, K2tog, SSK, K5, LT, K3 (7, 11). 46 (54, 62) sts.
Rnd 23: K3 (7, 11), Sl1, K38, Sl1, K3 (7, 11).
Rnd 24: K2 (6, 10), RT, K6, (RL, K2, LL, K4) four times, RL, K2, LL, K6, LT, K2 (6, 10). 56 (64, 72) sts.
Rnd 25: K2 (6, 10), Sl1, K50, Sl1, K2 (6, 10).
Rnd 26: K1 (5, 9), RT, K50, LT, K1 (5, 9).
Rnd 27: K1 (5, 9), Sl1, (K4, K2tog, SSK) six times, K4, Sl1, K1 (5, 9). 44 (52, 60) sts.
Rnd 28: K0 (4, 8), RT, K40, LT, K0 (4, 8).

Size 7 (-, -)" Only (Leg Traverse)
Rnd 29: Sl1, K5, (RL, K2, LL, K4) five times, RL, K2, LL, K5, Sl1 to CN, remove BOR M, K1, PM for BOR, Sl st from CN to LH needle. 56 sts.

Sizes - (8, 9)" Only (Leg Traverse)
Rnd 29: K- (4, 8), Sl1, K5, (RL, K2, LL, K4) five times, RL, K2, LL, K5, Sl1, K- (4, 8). - (64, 72) sts.
Rnd 30: K- (3, 7), RT, K54, LT, K- (3, 7).
Rnd 31: K- (3, 7), Sl1, K56, Sl1, K- (3, 7).
Rnd 32: K- (2, 6), RT, K2, (K2tog, SSK, K4) six times, K2tog, SSK, K2, LT, K- (2, 6). - (50, 58) sts.
Rnd 33: K- (2, 6), Sl1, K44, Sl1, K- (2, 6).
Rnd 34: K- (1, 5), RT, K3, (RL, K2, LL, K4) six times, RL, K2, LL, K3, LT, K- (1, 5). - (64, 72) sts.
Rnd 35: K- (1, 5), Sl1, K60, Sl1, K- (1, 5).
Rnd 36: K- (0, 4), RT, K60, LT, K- (0, 4).

Size - (8, -)" Only (Leg Traverse)
Rnd 37: Sl1, K1, (K2tog, SSK, K4) seven times, K2tog, SSK, K1, Sl1 to CN, remove BOR M, K1, PM for BOR, Sl st from CN to LH needle. 48 sts.

Size - (-, 9)" Only (Leg Traverse)
Rnd 37: K4, Sl1, K1, (K2tog, SSK, K4) seven times, K2tog, SSK, K1, Sl1, K4. 56 sts.
Rnd 38: K3, RT, K46, LT, K3.
Rnd 39: K3, Sl1, K2, (RL, K2, LL, K4) seven times, RL, K2, LL, K2, Sl11, K3. 72 sts.
Rnd 40: K2, RT, K64, LT, K2.
Rnd 41: K2, Sl1, K66, Sl1, K2.
Rnd 42: K1, RT, K1, (SSK, K4, K2tog) eight times, K1, LT, K1. 56 sts.
Rnd 43: K1, Sl1, K52, Sl1, K1.
Rnd 44: RT, K3, (LL, K4, RL, K2) seven times, LL, K4, RL, K3, LT. 72 sts.
Rnd 45: Sl1, K70, Sl1.

Leg Pattern (in the round beginning over a multiple of 8 sts)
Rnds 1–2: K all. 8 sts per rep.
Rnd 3: K2, K2tog, SSK, K2. 6 sts per rep.
Rnd 4: K all.
Rnd 5: K2, RL, K2, LL, K2. 8 sts per rep.
Rnds 6–7: K all.
Rnd 8: SSK, K4, K2tog. 6 sts per rep.
Rnd 9: K all.
Rnd 10: K1, LL, K4, RL, K1. 8 sts per rep.
Rep Rnds 1–10 for pattern.

DIRECTIONS

Toe
Using Judy's Magic Cast On, cast on 16 (20, 24) sts; 8 (10, 12) sts on each needle. PM for BOR.
Knit one rnd.
Inc Rnd: On Needle 1, *K1, M1L, K to last st, M1R, K1; rep from * on Needle 2. 4 sts inc.
Rep Inc Rnd four more times. 36 (40, 44) sts.
Next Rnd: K all.
Rep the last two rnds 5 (6, 7) more times. 56 (64, 72) sts; 28 (32, 36) sts on each needle.

Foot
Work St st for 27 (29, 32) rnds or until foot measures approx 4 (4.75, 5.25)" shorter than desired foot length.

Instep & Gusset
Rnd 1: K12 (14, 16), PM, K4, PM, K to end.
Rnd 2: K to M, SM, work in Instep Pattern from chart or written instructions to M, K to end.
Rep Rnd 2 until pattern Rnds 1–26 (30, 34) have been worked. 78 (84, 94) sts.
Setup for Heel Turn: K to M, work Rnd 27 (31, 35) of Instep Pattern, K12 (K14, 16). 80 (92, 96) sts.

Heel Turn
Heel turn is worked back and forth in rows on Needle 2 only, using German Short Rows with double stitches (DS).
Short Row 1 (RS): K28 (32, 36), turn.
Short Row 2 (WS): Make DS, P27 (31, 35), turn.
Short Row 3: Make DS, K to last st before DS, turn.
Short Row 4: Make DS, P to last st before DS, turn.
Rep Short Rows 3–4 another 7 (8, 10) times.
Next Short Row (RS): Make DS, K to end of needle being careful to catch both strands for all DSs, turn.
Next Short Row (WS): Sl1 WYIF, P to end of needle being careful to catch both strands for all DSs, turn.

Heel Flap
Heel flap is worked back and forth in rows and is joined with gusset sts at end of each row with decs. Rearrange sts before working heel flap, transfering first 12 (14, 16) sts and last 12 (14, 16) sts of Needle 1 to Needle 2. Adjust sts so first st to work is last st just worked for heel.
Short Row 1 (RS): Sl1 WYIB, K26 (30, 34), SSK. 1 gusset st dec.
Short Row 2 (WS): Sl1 WYIF, P26 (30, 34), P2tog, turn. 1 gusset st dec.
Rep Short Rows 1–2 another 11 (13, 15) times. 56 (64, 64) sts.
Setup Partial Row for Leg (RS): Sl1 WYIB, K13 (15, 17), PM for BOR.

Leg Section 1
Begin working in the rnd again.
Rnd 1: Work in Leg Traverse Pattern for your size from written instructions or chart, starting on Rnd 1 (5, 9).
Rep Rnd 1 until Rnd 29 (36, 44) of pattern has been completed.
Next Rnd: Work Rnd 30 (37, 45) to last st, place st on CN, remove M, K1, PM for BOR and place st from CN onto LH needle.

Leg Section 2

Rnd 1: Work Rnd 1 (4, 7) in Leg Pattern from written instructions or chart 7 (8, 9) times around.

Rnd 2: Work next rnd in Leg Pattern.

Rep Rnd 2 another 20 (22, 24) times, ending with Rnd 2 (7, 2) of Leg Pattern.

Cuff

Work Twisted Rib for 16 rnds.
BO in pattern using Jeny's Surprisingly Stretchy Bind Off.

Second Sock

Make second sock same as first.

Finishing

Weave in ends, wash, and block as desired.

LEGEND

■	**No Stitch** Placeholder—no stitch made
□	**Knit Stitch**
V	**Sl** Slip stitch purl-wise, with yarn in back
╱	**K2tog** Knit 2 stitches together as one stitch
╲	**SSK** Slip, slip, knit slipped stitches together
↱	**M1R** Make 1 right-leaning stitch
↰	**M1L** Make 1 left-leaning stitch
↓	**LL** Left-leaning loop (see *Notes* for instructions)
↓	**RL** Right-leaning loop (see *Notes* for instructions)

Leg Chart

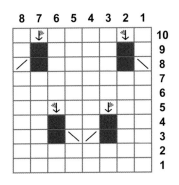

Instep Chart

LEGEND (CONTINUED)

Right Twist (RT)
Sl1 to CN, hold in back; K1, K1 from CN

Left Twist (LT)
Sl1 to CN, hold in front; K1, K1 from CN

Size 7"

Size 8"

Size 9"

Leg Traverse Chart

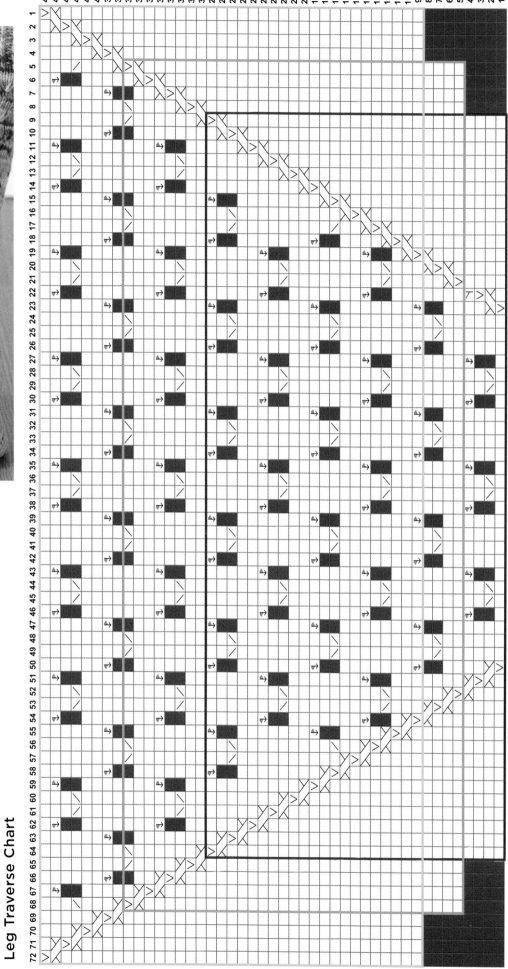

INTERLINK
by Sandi Rosner

FINISHED MEASUREMENTS

7.25 (8, 8.75, 9.5)" leg circumference ×
8.25 (8.75, 9.5, 10)" foot length, meant to
be worn with approx 10% negative ease

YARN

Stroll™ Hand Painted (fingering weight,
75% Fine Superwash Merino Wool, 25%
Nylon; 462 yards/100g): Hummingbird
28274, 1 (1, 1, 2) hanks

NEEDLES

US 1 (2.25mm) DPNs or two circular
needles for two circulars technique or
32" or longer circular needles for Magic
Loop technique, or size to obtain gauge

NOTIONS

Yarn Needle
Stitch Markers
Scrap Yarn or Stitch Holder

GAUGE

40 sts and 50 rnds = 4" in Interlink
Pattern, blocked
36 sts and 48 rnds = 4" in Stockinette
Stitch in the round, blocked

For pattern support, contact rosnersandi@gmail.com

Interlink

Notes:

The linked diamonds in this stitch pattern are reminiscent of fishnets or chain-link fences. It brings a lovely texture to the ankles and tops of the feet, while Stockinette Stitch keeps the soles and toes comfortable.

The Interlink Socks are knit in the round from the cuff to the toes, with a flap-and-gusset heel. The Interlink pattern on the leg extends down the top of the foot, while the heel, sole, and toe are worked in Stockinette Stitch.

Chart is worked in the round; read each chart row from right to left as a RS row.

LT (Left Twist)
Sl1 st K-wise, Sl a second st K-wise, Sl both sts back to LH needle in their new orientation; reach behind the first st to K into the back of the second st, then K into the back of both sts tog and Sl both sts off LH needle.

RT (Right Twist)
K2tog leaving the sts on the LH needle, then K the first st only and Sl both sts off LH needle.

Interlink Pattern (in the round over a multiple of 8 sts)
Rnd 1: (K1, RT, K2, LT, K1) to end.
Rnd 2: K all.
Rnd 3: (RT, K4, LT) to end.
Rnd 4: K all.
Rnd 5: (K1, LT, K2, RT, K1) to end.
Rnd 6: K all.
Rnd 7: (K2, LT, RT, K2) to end.
Rnd 8: K all.
Rep Rnds 1–8 for pattern.

2x2 Rib (in the round over a multiple of 4 sts)
Rnd 1: P1, (K2, P2) to last 3 sts, K2, P1.
Rep Rnd 1 for pattern.

DIRECTIONS

Cuff
Loosely CO 72 (80, 88, 96) sts.
Join to work in the rnd, being careful not to twist sts; PM for BOR.
Work 2x2 Rib for 18 rnds.

Leg
Work Interlink Pattern until piece measures approx 6.5 (7, 7.5, 8)" from CO edge, ending with an even-numbered rnd.

Divide for Heel
Setup Rnd: Work 32 (40, 40, 48) sts in Interlink Pattern and place these sts on scrap yarn or st holder for instep, K3 (3, 4, 4), K2tog, *K7 (7, 9, 9), K2tog; rep from * two more times, K to end. 36 (36, 44, 44) sts remain for heel.

Heel Flap
Working back and forth in rows, work St st until flap measures 1.75 (2, 2.25, 2.5)" from division, ending with a RS row.

Heel Turn
Short Row 1 (WS): Sl1 WYIF, P18 (18, 22, 22), P2tog, P1, turn.
Short Row 2 (RS): Sl1 WYIB, K3, SSK, K1, turn.
Short Row 3: Sl1 WYIF, P to 1 st before gap caused by last turn, P2tog to close gap, P1, turn.
Short Row 4: Sl1 WYIB, K to 1 st before gap caused by last turn, SSK to close gap, K1, turn.
Rep Short Rows 3–4 another 6 (6, 9, 9) times. 20 (20, 22, 22) sts.

Gusset
Setup Rnd: PU and K 16 (18, 20, 22) sts along side edge of heel flap, PM, work next rnd of Interlink Pattern over held sts for instep, PM, PU and K 16 (18, 20, 22) sts along other side edge of heel flap, K10 (10, 11, 11) to center of heel; PM for BOR. 84 (96, 102, 114) sts.
Rnd 1: K to first M, work Interlink Pattern to next M, K to end.
Rnd 2: K to 3 sts before first M, K2tog, K1, SM, work Interlink Pattern to next M, SM, K1, SSK, K to end. 2 sts dec.
Rep Rnds 1–2 another 7 (9, 8, 10) times. 68 (76, 84, 92) sts.

Foot
Rnd 1: K to first M, work Interlink Pattern to next M, K to end.
Rep Rnd 1 until foot measures 2.25 (2.5, 2.75, 3)" shorter than desired finished length.

Toe
Sizes 7.25 (-, 8.75, -)" Only
Setup Rnd: K16 (-, 20, -), PM, K2, remove M, K3 (-, 4 -), *K2tog, K6 (-, 8, -); rep from * two more times, K2tog, K3 (-, 4 -), remove M, K2, PM, K to end. 64 (-, 80, -) sts.

Sizes - (8, -, 9.5)" Only
Setup Rnd: K to first M, SM, K- (4, -, 5), *K2tog, K- (8, -, 10); rep from * two more times, K2tog, K- (4, -, 5), SM, K to end. - (72, -, 88) sts.

Resume All Sizes
Rnd 1: (K to 3 sts before M, K2tog, K1, SM, K1, SSK) two times, K to end. 4 sts dec.
Rnd 2: K all.
Rep Rnds 1–2 another 11 (12, 14, 16) times. 16 (20, 20, 20) sts.
Rep Rnd 1 another 2 (3, 3, 3) times. 8 sts.
Remove BOR M, K2.
Graft toe closed using Kitchener Stitch.

Second Sock
Make second sock same as first.

Finishing
Weave in ends. Wash and block as desired.

Interlink Chart

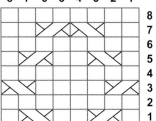

LEGEND

☐ **Knit Stitch**

⬚ **Right Twist (RT)**
Sl1 to CN, hold in back; K1, K1 from CN
(or see *Notes* to work withouth a CN)

⬚ **Left Twist (LT)**
Sl1 to CN, hold in front; K1, K1 from CN
(or see *Notes* to work withouth a CN)

JIVE
by Katie Noseworthy

FINISHED MEASUREMENTS
7 (7.5, 8, 8.5, 9)" leg circumference

YARN
Hawthorne™ (fingering weight, 80%
Fine Superwash Highland Wool, 20%
Polyamide (Nylon); 357 yards/100g):
Happy Valley 26441, 1 hank

NEEDLES
US 2 (2.75mm) DPNs or two circular
needles for two circulars technique or
32" or longer circular needles for Magic
Loop technique, or size to obtain gauge

NOTIONS
Yarn Needle
Stitch Markers
Cable Needle

GAUGE
30 sts and 48 rnds = 4" in Stockinette
Stitch, blocked

For pattern support, contact katie.noseworthy@gmail.com

Jive

Notes:

These socks were made for swinging! Inspired by the rambunctious sounds of jazz, the Jive socks have been specially designed with the wildest of variegated yarns in mind—breaking up colors but showing them off all at the same time.

These socks use slipped stitches and small cables to create a striking texture. The front and instep feature an angular design, whereas the back of the leg complements this with alternating columns. The socks are constructed with a traditional heel flap design and are worked top down. Knit, wear, dance!

Chart is worked in the round; read each chart row from right to left as a RS row.

RT (Right Twist)
Sl1 to CN, hold in back; K1, K1 from CN.

LT (Left Twist)
Sl1 to CN, hold in front; K1, K1 from CN.

Chart A (in the round over 29 sts)
Rnd 1: (K1, LT) three times, K11, (RT, K1) three times.
Rnd 2: (K2, Sl1) three times, K11, (Sl1, K2) three times.
Rnd 3: K2, LT, (K1, LT) two times, K9, (RT, K1) three times, K1.
Rnd 4: K3, Sl1, (K2, Sl1) two times, K9, (Sl1, K2) two times, Sl1, K3.
Rnd 5: K3, LT, (K1, LT) two times, K7, (RT, K1) two times, RT, K3.
Rnd 6: K4, Sl1, (K2, Sl1) two times, K7, (Sl1, K2) two times, Sl1, K4.
Rnd 7: (K1, LT) four times, K5, (RT, K1) four times.
Rnd 8: (K2, Sl1) four times, K5, (Sl1, K2) four times.
Rnd 9: K2, LT, (K1, LT) three times, K3, (RT, K1) three times, RT, K2.
Rnd 10: K3, Sl1, (K2, Sl1) three times, K3, (Sl1, K2) three times, Sl1, K3.
Rnd 11: K3, LT, (K1, LT) three times, (K1, RT) four times, K3.
Rnd 12: K4, Sl1, (K2, Sl1) three times, K1, (Sl1, K2) three times, Sl1, K4.
Rnd 13: K3, RT, (K1, RT) three times, (K1, LT) four times, K3.
Rnd 14: K3, Sl1, (K2, Sl1) three times, K3, (Sl1, K2) three times, Sl1, K3.
Rnd 15: K2, RT, (K1, RT) three times, K3, (LT, K1) three times, LT, K2.
Rnd 16: (K2, Sl1) four times, K5, (Sl1, K2) four times.
Rnd 17: (K1, RT) four times, K5, (LT, K1) four times.
Rnd 18: K1, Sl1, (K2, Sl1) three times, K7, (Sl1, K2) three times, Sl1, K1.
Rnd 19: K3, RT, (K1, RT) two times, K7, (LT, K1) two times, LT, K3.
Rnd 20: K3, Sl1, (K2, Sl1) two times, K9, (Sl1, K2) two times, Sl1, K3.
Rnd 21: K2, RT, (K1, RT) two times, K9, (LT, K1) two times, LT, K2.
Rnd 22: (K2, Sl1) three times, K11, (Sl1, K2) three times.
Rnd 23: (K1, RT) three times, K11, (LT, K1) three times.
Rnd 24: K1, Sl1, (K2, Sl1) two times, K13, (Sl1, K2) two times, Sl1, K1.
Rnd 25: K3, RT, K1, RT, K13, LT, K1, LT, K3.

Rnd 26: K3, Sl1, K2, Sl1, K15, Sl1, K2, Sl1, K3.
Rnd 27: K2, RT, K1, RT, K15, LT, K1, LT, K2.
Rnd 28: (K2, Sl1) two times, K17, (Sl1, K2) two times.
Rnd 29: (K1, RT) two times, K17, (LT, K1) two times.
Rnd 30: K4, Sl1, K19, Sl1, K4.
Rnd 31: K3, RT, K19, LT, K3.
Rnd 32: K3, Sl1, K21, Sl1, K3.
Rnd 33: K2, RT, K21, LT, K2.
Rnd 34: K2, Sl1, K23, Sl1, K2.
Rnd 35: K1, RT, K23, LT, K1.
Rep Rnds 1–24 for pattern.

DIRECTIONS

Cuff
CO 62 (66, 70, 74, 78) sts using the Long-Tail Cast On.
Join to work in the rnd and PM for BOR.

Sizes 7 (-, 8, -, 9)" Only
Rnds 1–18: (P1, K1 TBL) to end.

Sizes - (7.5, -, 8.5, -)" Only
Rnds 1–18: (K1 TBL, P1) to end.

Leg
The leg is worked using a combination for Chart A (from chart or written instructions above) and written instructions below. Follow the instructions for your size below.

Size 7" Only
Setup Rnd: P1, K29, P1, PM, K1, P1, (K3, P1, K1, P1) four times, K3, P1, K1.
Rnd 1: P1, work Rnd 1 of Chart A, P1, K1, P1, (K3, P1, K1, P1) four times, K3, P1, K1.
Rnd 2: P1, work next rnd of Chart A, P1, Sl1, P1, (K3, P1, Sl1, P1) four times, K3, P1, Sl1.

Size 7.5" Only
Setup Rnd: K1, P1, K29, P1, K1, PM, (P1, K1, P1, K3) five times, P1, K1, P1.
Rnd 1: K1, P1, work Rnd 1 of Chart A, P1, K1, (P1, K1, P1, K3) five times, P1, K1.
Rnd 2: Sl1, P1, work next rnd of Chart A, P1, Sl1, (P1, Sl1, P1, K3) five times, P1, Sl1.

Size 8" Only
Setup Rnd: P1, K1, P1, K29, P1, K1, P1, PM, K1, (P1, K1, P1, K3) five times, (P1, K1) two times.
Rnd 1: P1, K1, P1, work Rnd 1 of Chart A, P1, K1, P1, K1, (P1, K1, P1, K3) five times, (P1, K1) two times.
Rnd 2: P1, Sl1, P1, work next rnd of Chart A, P1, Sl1, P1, Sl1, (P1, Sl1, P1, K3) five times, (P1, Sl1) two times.

Size 8.5" Only
Setup Rnd: (K1, P1) two times, K29, (P1, K1) two times, PM, K2, (P1, K1, P1, K3) five times, P1, K1, K2.
Rnd 1: (K1, P1), two times, work Rnd 1 of Chart A, (P1, K1) two times, K2, (P1, K1, P1, K3) five times, P1, K1, P1, K2.

Rnd 2: K1, P1, Sl1, P1, work next rnd of Chart A, P1, Sl1, P1, K3, (P1, Sl1, P1, K3) five times, P1, Sl1, P1, K2.

Size 9" Only

Setup Rnd: P1, (K1, P1) two times, K29, (P1, K1) two times, P1, PM, K3, (P1, K1, P1, K3) five times, P1, K1, P1, K3.

Rnd 1: P1, (K1, P1) two times, work Rnd 1 of Chart A, (P1, K1) two times, P1, K3, (P1, K1, P1, K3) five times, P1, K1, P1, K3.

Rnd 2: P1, (Sl1, P1) two times, work next rnd of Chart A, (P1, Sl1) two times, P1, K3 (P1, Sl1, P1, K3) five times, P1, Sl1, P1, K3.

Resume All Sizes

Cont working as established, alternating written instructions for Rnds 1-2 through Rnd 24 of Chart A. Work Rnds 1-24 of Chart A two times total before beginning heel, or to desired length.

Heel Flap

Setup Rnd: Work across first 31 (33, 35, 37, 39) sts in pattern as established. Heel flap is worked flat across next 31 (33, 35, 37, 39) sts as follows.

Row 1 (RS): Sl1 WYIB, K0 (0, 0, 1, 2), P0 (0, 1, 1, 1), K0 (1, 1, 1, 1), (P1, K1, Sl1, K1, P1, K1) five times, P0 (1, 1, 1, 1), K0 (0, 1, 2, 3), turn work.

Row 2 (WS): Sl1 WYIF, P0 (0, 0, 1, 2), K0 (0, 1, 1, 1), P0 (1, 1, 1, 1), (K1, P3, K1, P1) five times, K0 (1, 1, 1, 1), P0 (0, 1, 2, 3), turn work.
Rep Rows 1-2 until heel flap measures 2.25 (2.25, 2.5, 2.5, 2.75)" after a WS row.

Heel Turn

Short Row 1 (RS): Sl1 WYIB, K16 (17, 18, 19, 20), SSK, K1, turn.

Short Row 2 (WS): Sl1 WYIF, P5, P2tog, P1, turn.

Short Row 3: Sl1 WYIB, K6, SSK, K1, turn.

Short Row 4: Sl1 WYIF, P7, P2tog, P1, turn.
Rep Short Rows 3-4 until all heel sts have been worked.

Next Row: K across the turned heel sts, PU and K 1 st in each slipped st along right side of heel flap, PU and K 1 st between gusset and instep sts, PM for BOR.

Next Rnd: Work across 31 (33, 35, 37, 39) instep sts in established pattern, PM, PU and K 1 st between instep and gusset sts, PU and K 1 st in each slipped st along left side of heel flap, K to end.

Gusset

Rnd 1: Work as established across 31 (33, 35, 37, 39) instep sts to first M, SM, K1, SSK, K across gusset sts to last 3 sts, K2tog, K1. 2 sts dec.

Rnd 2: Work as established across 31 (33, 35, 37, 39) instep sts, SM, K to end.
Rep Rnds 1-2 until 31 (33, 35, 37, 39) sts remain for sole. 62 (66, 70, 74, 78) sts total.

Foot

Foot is worked in established pattern for the 31 (33, 35, 37, 39) instep sts, and in St st for the 31 (33, 35, 37, 39) sole sts. Cont working in this manner through end of Chart A.

When to Stop Working Chart A

The sock is designed so pattern on foot ends after Rnd 35 of Chart A. Each time you complete Rnd 24, check length to make sure there is enough length remaining to fit another rep of Chart A Rnds 1-24.

When foot measures 5" shorter than desired length, work Chart A Rnds 25-35 as established.

After finishing Chart A Rnd 35, work as follows until foot measures approx 2.5" shorter than desired length.

Size 7": P1, K29, P1, K to end.
Size 7.5": K1, P1, K29, P1, K1, K to end.
Size 8": P1, K1, P1, K29, P1, K1, P1, K to end.
Size 8.5": (K1, P1) two times, K29, (P1, K1) two times, K to end.
Size 9": P1, (K1, P1) two times, K29, (P1, K1) two times, P1, K to end.

Toe

Toe decs are worked in established pattern, consuming the pattern as it is worked.

Rnd 1: P1 (0, 1, 0, 1), K0 (1, 0, 1, 0), SSK, work as established to 3 sts before M, K2tog, P1 (0, 1, 0, 1), K0 (1, 0, 1, 0), SM, K1, SSK, K to last 3 sts, K2tog, K1. 4 sts dec.

Rnd 2: WE as established.
Rep Rnds 1-2 until 22 (22, 22, 26, 26) sts remain, or until toe reaches desired length.
Graft toe closed using Kitchener Stitch.

Second Sock

Make second sock same as first.

Finishing

Weave in all ends using a tapestry needle.
Block, using sock blockers if desired.

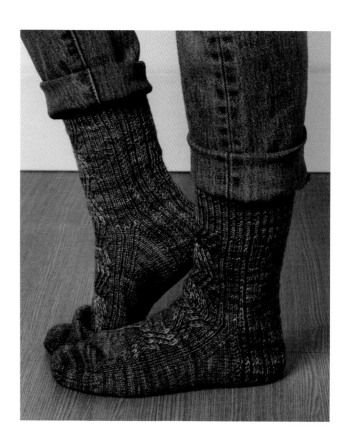

LEGEND

☐ Knit Stitch

Ⅴ **Sl**
Slip stitch purl-wise, with yarn in back

▱ **Right Twist (RT)**
Sl1 to CN, hold in back; K1, K1 from CN

◹ **Left Twist (LT)**
Sl1 to CN, hold in front; K1, K1 from CN

☐ **Pattern Repeat**

Jive Chart

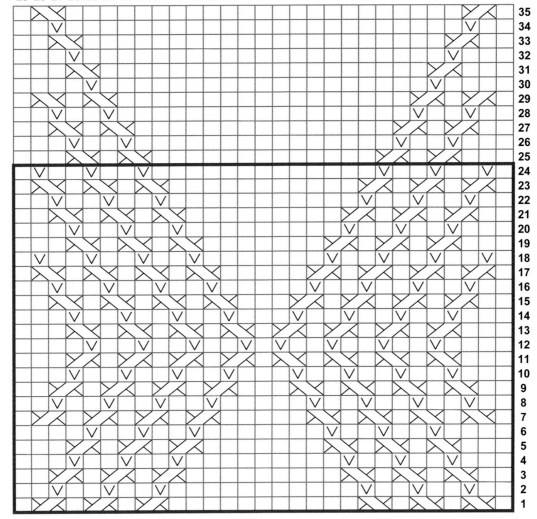

LIANA
by Aud Bergo

FINISHED MEASUREMENTS

6 (6.75, 7.5, 8)" foot circumference ×
8.5 (8.75, 9.25, 9.75)" foot length, to fit
US shoe sizes 7 (8, 8.5, 9.5); meant to
be worn with approx 1.5–2" negative
ease (foot length is adjustable)

YARN

Stroll™ Tonal (fingering weight, 75% Fine
Superwash Merino Wool, 25% Nylon;
462 yards/100g): Manatee 28265, 1 hank

NEEDLES

US 2 (2.75mm) 32" circular needles for
Magic Loop technique or DPNs or two
24" for two circular technique, or size
to obtain gauge

US 1 (2.25mm) 32" circular needles for
Magic Loop technique or DPNs or two
24" for two circular technique, or one
size smaller than size used to obtain gauge

NOTIONS

Yarn Needle
Stitch Markers
Cable Needle

GAUGE

56 sts and 42 rnds = 4" in Liana Pattern
in the round, relaxed and unblocked (note
that this is approximate due to the
amount of stretch in the pattern)
32 sts and 42 rnds = 4" in Stockinette
Stitch in the round, unblocked

For pattern support, contact audbergo@hotmail.com

Liana

Notes:

The Liana Socks are inspired by the climbing woody plant from our precious tropical forests. Imagine the Liana plant climbing and swirling around trees in a rainforest providing valuable habitat for animals and insects in the forest canopy.

After a short cuff, the pattern starts with ribbing on these top-down socks. A slip-stitch heel flap and traditional gusset are used. The Liana pattern is worked on the instep, while the sole is knit in Stockinette Stitch.

The Liana pattern has quite a lot of stretch and is meant to be worn with approx 1.5–2″ negative ease. The pattern looks best if the ease is not too large, so consider going up a size rather than making a smaller size with more negative ease.

For the largest size, consider buying an extra hank of yarn, as there will be hardly any leftover yarn.

Instructions are given for Magic Loop or two circular needles technique, but can be easily adjusted to DPNs by dividing stitches on each needle across two DPNs.

All rnds begin with front leg/instep (Needle 1), followed by back leg back/gusset/sole (Needle 2).

A smaller needle size is used for cuff, heel, and toe. This adds durability to the heel and toe, and a nice transition from cuff to Liana pattern on leg.

Chart is worked in the round; read each chart row from right to left as a RS row.

1/3 RC (1 over 3 Right Cable)
Sl3 to CN, hold in back; K1, K3 from CN.

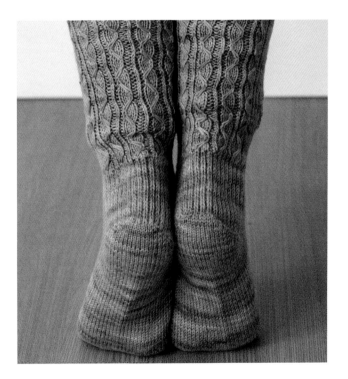

1/3 LC (1 over 3 Left Cable)
Sl1 to CN, hold in front; K3, K1 from CN.

Liana Pattern (in the round over a multiple of 7 sts)
Rnd 1: K1 TBL, P1, K4, P1.
Rnd 2: Rep Rnd 1.
Rnd 3: K1 TBL, P1, Sl1, K3, P1.
Rnd 4: Rep Rnd 3.
Rnd 5: K1 TBL, P1, 1/3 LC, P1.
Rnds 6–7: Rep Rnd 1.
Rnd 8: K1 TBL, P1, K3, Sl1, P1.
Rnd 9: Rep Rnd 8.
Rnd 10: K1 TBL, P1, 1/3 RC, P1.
Rep Rnds 1–10 for pattern.

DIRECTIONS

Cuff
Using smaller needles, CO 64 (70, 78, 84) sts.
Distribute sts as follows: Leg Front, Needle 1—31 (34, 38, 41) sts; Leg Back, Needle 2—33 (36, 40, 43) sts.

Join to work in the rnd, being careful not to twist sts; PM for BOR.

Sizes 6 (-, 7.5, -)″ Only
Rnd 1: Needle 1—P1, (K1 TBL, P2, K2, P2) 4 (5) times, K1 TBL, P1; Needle 2—K1 TBL, P1, (K1 TBL, P2, K2, P2) 4 (5) times, K1 TBL, P1, K1 TBL.

Sizes - (6.75, -, 8)″ Only
Rnd 1: Needle 1—P2, K2, P2, (K1 TBL, P2, K2, P2) 4 (5) times; Needle 2—(K1 TBL, P2, K2, P2) 5 (6) times, K1 TBL.

Resume All Sizes
Rep Rnd 1 five more times.

Leg
Change to larger needles.

Sizes 6 (-, 7.5, -)″ Only
Rnds 1–10: Needle 1—P1, work Liana Pattern from chart or written instructions 4 (-, 5, -) times, K1 TBL, P1; Needle 2—K1 TBL, P1, work Liana Pattern 4 (-, 5, -) times, K1 TBL, P1, K1 TBL.

Sizes - (6.75, -, 8)″ Only
Rnds 1–2: Needle 1—P1, K4, P1, work Liana Pattern from chart or written instructions - (4, -, 5) times; Needle 2—work Liana Pattern - (5, -, 6) times, K1 TBL.
Rnds 3–4: Needle 1—P1, Sl1, K3, P1, work Liana Pattern - (4, -, 5) times; Needle 2—work Liana Pattern - (5, -, 6) times, K1 TBL.
Rnd 5: Needle 1—P1, 1/3 LC, P1, work Liana Pattern - (4, -, 5) times; Needle 2—work Liana Pattern - (5, -, 6) times, K1 TBL.
Rnds 6–7: Rep Rnds 1–2.
Rnds 8–9: Needle 1—P1, K3, Sl1, P1, work Liana Pattern - (4, -, 5) times; Needle 2—work Liana Pattern - (5, -, 6) times, K1 TBL.
Rnd 10: Needle 1—P1, 1/3 RC, P1, work Liana Pattern - (4, -, 5) times; Needle 2—work Liana Pattern - (5, -, 6) times, K1 TBL.

Resume All Sizes
Rep Rnds 1–10 another 5 (5, 5, 6) times. Remove M.

Heel Flap

The heel flap is worked back and forth on Needle 2 only. Change to smaller needles. Turn work to start on WS.

Sizes 6 (-, -, 8)" Only
Setup Row (WS): Sl1 WYIF, P16 (21), M1P, P16 (21). 34 (-, -, 44) sts.

Sizes - (6.75, 7.5, -)" Only
Setup Row (WS): P all heel sts.

Resume All Sizes
Row 1 (RS): (Sl1 WYIB, K1) to end.
Row 2 (WS): Sl1 WYIF, P to end.
Rep Rows 1–2 another 17 (18, 19, 20) times.
Work Row 1 once more. Flap measures approx 2.25 (2.5, 2.5, 2.75)".

Heel Turn

Short Row 1 (WS): Sl1 WYIF, P18 (20, 22, 24), P2tog, P1, turn. 1 st dec.
Short Row 2 (RS): Sl1 WYIB, K5 (7, 7, 7), SSK, K1, turn. 1 st dec.
Short Row 3: Sl1 WYIF, P to 1 st before gap, P2tog, P1, turn. 1 st dec.
Short Row 4: Sl1 WYIB, K to 1 st before gap, SSK, K1, turn. 1 st dec.
Rep Short Rows 3–4 until all sts before gaps are worked. 20 (22, 24, 26) heel sts. Do not turn on last row.

Gusset

The gusset is formed by picking up sts on each side of the heel flap and working across sole sts. Gusset and sole sts are Stockinette Stitch. Change to larger needles.
Left Gusset Setup Partial Rnd: With RS facing, PU and K 17 (18, 19, 21) sts along left side of heel flap, PM for BOR and resume working in the rnd.
Right Gusset Setup Rnd: Needle 1—work Liana Pattern as established; Needle 2—PU and K 17 (18, 19, 21) sts along right side of heel flap, K to end of rnd. 31 (34, 38, 41) sts on Needle 1; 54 (58, 62, 68) sts on Needle 2; 85 (92, 100, 109) sts total.

Sizes 6 (-, -, 8)" Only
Rnd 1: Needle 1—work Liana Pattern as established; Needle 2—K26 (-, -, 33) K2tog, K26 (-, -, 33). 1 st dec.

Sizes - (6.75, 7.5, -)" Only
Rnd 1: Needle 1—work Liana Pattern as established; Needle 2—K to end.

Resume All Sizes
Rnd 2: Needle 1—work Liana Pattern as established; Needle 2—SSK, K to last 2 sts, K2tog. 2 sts dec.
Rnd 3: Needle 1—work as established; Needle 2—K all.
Rnd 4: Needle 1—work as established; Needle 2—SSK, K to last 2 sts, K2tog. 2 sts dec.
Rep Rnds 3–4 another 9 (10, 10, 11) times until 31 (34, 38, 41) sts remain on Needle 2.

Foot

Cont working sole in St st and instep pattern as established until foot measures 1.5 (1.75, 2, 2)" shorter than desired length, measured from back of heel to live sts. End on stitch pattern Rnd 1, 2, 5, 6, 7, or 10.

Toe

Change to smaller needles.
Rnd 1: K all.
Rnd 2: Needle 1—K1, SSK, K to last 3 sts, K2tog, K1; Needle 2— work same as for Needle 1. 2 sts dec each needle, 4 sts dec total.
Rep Rnds 1–2 four more times until 42 (48, 56, 62) sts remain total.
Rep Rnd 2 until 14 (12, 12, 14) sts remain.

Break yarn, leaving a 15" tail.
With tail threaded onto a yarn needle, graft sts closed using Kitchener Stitch. Alternatively, thread tail through sts, pulling tight to close hole. Fasten off.

Second Sock

Make second sock same as first.

Finishing

Weave in ends, wash, and block as desired.

Liana Pattern

7	6	5	4	3	2	1	
•	⟍ 1/3 RC				•	Q	10
•	V				•	Q	9
•	V				•	Q	8
•					•	Q	7
•					•	Q	6
•	⟋ 1/3 LC				•	Q	5
•			V		•	Q	4
•			V		•	Q	3
•					•	Q	2
•					•	Q	1

LEGEND

☐ **Knit Stitch**

• **Purl Stitch**

Q **K TBL**
Knit stitch through the back loop

V **Sl**
Slip stitch purl-wise, with yarn in back

 1 over 3 Right Cable (1/3 RC)
Sl3 to CN, hold in back; K1, K3 from CN

 1 over 3 Left Cable (1/3 LC)
Sl1 to CN, hold in front; K3, K1 from CN

NOUVEAU
by Katy Banks

FINISHED MEASUREMENTS

7.25 (8, 8.75)" finished foot circumference; meant to be worn with 5–10% negative ease

YARN

Hawthorne™ (fingering weight, 80% Fine Superwash Highland Wool, 20% Polymide (Nylon); 357 yards/100g): Spark Speckle 28618, 2 hanks

NEEDLES

US 1 (2.25mm) DPNs or two circular needles for two circulars technique or 32" or longer circular needles for Magic Loop technique, or size to obtain gauge

NOTIONS

Yarn Needle
Stitch Markers
Cable Needle or spare DPN
Scrap Yarn or Stitch Holder

GAUGE

40 sts and 56 rnds = 4" in Hourglass Pattern in the round, blocked
34 sts and 56 rnds = 4" in Stockinette Stitch in the round, blocked

For pattern support, contact katybanksdesigns@gmail.com

Nouveau

Notes:

Inspired by the art movement for which the pattern is named, these socks pull together stitch patterns reminiscent of the sinuous curves found in nature. The asymmetrical pattern placement allows the sock to hug the curve of the lower leg.

Nouveau Socks are worked from the top down with a heel flap and gusset construction. The cables open into the hourglass pattern that continues down the heel flap and across the top of the foot. The stitch count difference between the cables and the hourglass sections create natural calf shaping.

Always slip stitches purl-wise with yarn held to wrong side.

Charts are worked both in the round and flat. When working chart in the round, read each chart row from right to left as a RS row; when working chart flat, read RS rows (even numbers) from right to left, and WS rows (odd numbers) from left to right.

1/2 RC (1 over 2 Right Cable)
Sl2 to CN, hold in back; K1, K2 from CN.

LPT (Left Twist, Purl back)
Sl1 to CN, hold in front; P1, K1 from CN.

RPT (Right Twist, Purl back)
Sl1 to CN, hold in back; K1, P1 from CN.

RCD (Right Cable Decrease)
Sl2 to CN, hold in back; K1, K2tog from CN. 1 st dec.

Cable Pattern (in the round over a multiple of 5 sts)
Rnd 1: (K3, P2) to end.
Rnd 2: (K2, Sl1, P2) to end.
Rnd 3: Rep Rnd 2.
Rnd 4: (1/2 RC, P2) to end.
Rep Rnds 1-4 for pattern.

Hourglass Pattern (in the round over a multiple of 8 sts)
Rnd 1: (Sl1, P6, Sl1) to end.
Rnd 2: (K1, P6, K1) to end.
Rnds 3-4: Rep Rnds 1-2.
Rnd 5: Rep Rnd 1.
Rnd 6: (LPT, P4, RPT) to end.
Rnd 7: (P1, Sl1, P4, Sl1, P1) to end.
Rnd 8: (P1, LPT, P2, RPT, P1) to end.
Rnd 9: (P2, Sl1, P2, Sl1, P2) to end.
Rnd 10: (P2, LPT, RPT, P2) to end.
Rnd 11: (P3, Sl2, P3) to end.
Rnd 12: (P3, K2, P3) to end.
Rnds 13-14: Rep Rnds 11-12.
Rnd 15: Rep Rnd 11.
Rnd 16: (P2, RPT, LPT, P2) to end.
Rnd 17: Rep Rnd 9.
Rnd 18: (P1, RPT, P2, LPT, P1) to end.
Rnd 19: Rep Rnd 7.
Rnd 20: (RPT, P4, LPT) to end.
Rep Rnds 1-20 for pattern.

Hourglass Pattern (flat over a multiple of 8 sts)
Rnd 1 (WS): (Sl1, K6, Sl1) to end.
Rnd 2 (RS): (K1, P6, K1) to end.
Rnds 3-4: Rep Rnds 1-2.
Rnd 5: Rep Rnd 1.
Rnd 6: (LPT, P4, RPT) to end.
Rnd 7: (K1, Sl1, K4, Sl1, K1) to end.
Rnd 8: (P1, LPT, P2, RPT, P1) to end.
Rnd 9: (K2, Sl1, K2, Sl1, K2) to end.
Rnd 10: (P2, LPT, RPT, P2) to end.
Rnd 11: (K3, Sl2, K3) to end.
Rnd 12: (P3, K2, P3) to end.
Rnds 13-14: Rep Rnds 11-12.
Rnd 15: Rep Rnd 11.
Rnd 16: (P2, RPT, LPT, P2) to end.
Rnd 17: Rep Rnd 9.
Rnd 18: (P1, RPT, P2, LPT, P1) to end.
Rnd 19: Rep Rnd 7.
Rnd 20: (RPT, P4, LPT) to end.
Rep Rnds 1-20 for pattern.

DIRECTIONS

Leg
Using stretchy method of choice, CO 90 (100, 110) sts.
PM for BOR. Join to work in the rnd.
Work Cable Pattern from chart or written instructions for seven rnds.

Setup Rnd: Work Cable Pattern as established for 35 (40, 45) sts, place "chart" M (M-A), cont in Cable Pattern for 10 sts, work RCD and place "center" M (M-B) between the resulting 2 sts, P2, cont in Cable Pattern for 8 sts, place "chart" M (M-C), P2, cont in Cable Pattern to end. New Ms denote where to work Charts 1 and 2, with "center" M (M-B) between them. 1 st dec.

Next Rnd: Work Cable Pattern to M-A, work Chart 1 to M-B, work Chart 2 to M-C, P2, work Cable Pattern to end.
Work through Rnd 20 of Charts 1 and 2 as established. 4 sts dec.

Next Rnd: Work Cable Pattern to 10 sts before M-A, place new "chart" M, work Chart 1, moving previously placed M-A ahead 1 st to new position; removing M-B as you go, work Hourglass Pattern to 1 st before M-C and move M-C 1 st back to new position, work Chart 2, place new "chart" M, P2, work Cable Pattern to end.
Work through Rnd 20 of Charts 1 and 2 as established. 4 sts dec.

Cont repeating Charts 1 and 2 in this manner, moving the placement further from center with each rep. After working Charts 1 and 2 a total of 4 (4, 5) times, only 1 (3, 1) cable(s) remain to be transitioned to Hourglass Pattern. 73 (83, 93) sts.

Chart 3 Notes: Be sure to use the Chart 3 option for your size. Chart 3 is arranged to be centered around BOR M, indicated with a red line.

Next Rnd: Work Chart 3 beginning at red line, working to end of chart row, place "chart" M; removing any other Ms as you go, work Hourglass Pattern to 1 st before last "chart" M placed previously and move this M 1 st back to new position, work first row of Chart 3 to red line (end of rnd). Cont working as established, through Chart 3 Rnd 8 (16, 8). Remove BOR M, Sl1, replace BOR M, cont working to end of Chart 3. Remove all "chart" Ms. 72 (80, 88) sts.

Next Rnd: Work Rnd 1 of Hourglass Pattern.

Heel Flap
Prepare differently for left sock or right sock.
Setup Rnd for Left Sock: Cont Hourglass Pattern in the rnd, working Rnd 2 for 32 (40, 40) sts, K2 (1, 2), turn work.
Setup Rnd for Right Sock: Cont Hourglass Pattern in the rnd, working Rnd 2 to end, K2 (1, 2), turn work.

Row 1 (WS): Sl1 WYIF, K1 (0, 1), (work Hourglass Pattern Row 3) to last 2 (1, 2) sts, K2 (1, 2), turn work (remove M).
Row 2 (RS): Sl1 WYIB, P1 (0, 1), (work Hourglass Pattern Row 4) to last 2 (1, 2) sts, P2 (1, 2).
Row 3: Sl1 WYIF, K1 (0, 1), (work next row of Hourglass Pattern) to last 2 (1, 2) sts, K2 (1, 2).
Row 4: Sl1 WYIB, P1 (0, 1), (work next row of Hourglass Pattern) to last 2 (1, 2) sts, P2 (1, 2).
Rows 5–18: Rep Rows 3–4 as established, working through Hourglass Pattern Row 20.
Row 19 (WS): Sl1 WYIF, K1 (0, 1), (work Hourglass Pattern Row 1) to last 2 (1, 2) sts, K2 (1, 2).
Row 20 (RS): Sl1 WYIB, P1 (0, 1), (work Hourglass Pattern Row 2) to last 2 (1, 2) sts, P2 (1, 2).
Work Rows 1–20 another 0 (1, 1) time, then work through Row 15 (1, 3) once more. 35 (41, 43) rows worked total.

Heel Turn
Short Row 1 (RS): K21 (25, 27), SSK, K1, turn.
Short Row 2 (WS): Sl1 WYIF, P7 (9, 11), P2tog, P1, turn.
Short Row 3: Sl1 WYIB, K to 1 st before gap, SSK, K1, turn.
Short Row 4: Sl1 WYIF, P to 1 st before gap, P2tog, P1, turn.
Rep Short Rows 3–4 until all heel sts have been worked, ending with a WS row. 22 (26, 28) heel sts remain.

Gusset
Gusset and sole are worked in Stockinette Stitch; instep will cont in Hourglass Pattern.

Setup Rnd for Left Sock: K across all heel sts, rotate work and PU and K 18 (21, 22) sts along heel flap selvage, PM before last 2 (1, 2) sts picked up, P5 (6, 5), K1, work Hourglass Pattern Rnd 2 across instep to last 6 (7, 6) sts, K1, P5 (6, 5), PU and K 18 (21, 22) sts along heel flap selvage, PM after first 2 (1, 2) sts picked up, K11 (13, 14), PM for BOR.

Setup Rnd for Right Sock: K across all heel sts, rotate work and PU and K 18 (21, 22) sts along heel flap selvage, PM before last 2 (1, 2) sts picked up, P5 (6, 5), Sl1, work Hourglass Pattern Rnd 3 across instep to last 6 (7, 6) sts, Sl1, P5 (6, 5), PU and K 18 (21, 22) sts along heel flap selvage, PM after first 2 (1, 2) sts picked up, K11 (13, 14), PM for BOR.

Resume Both Socks
There are 94 (106, 116) sts on needles: 27 (33, 34) heel and gusset sts, M, 40 (40, 48) instep sts, M, 27 (33, 34) gusset and heel sts.
Rnd 1: K to 2 sts before M, K2tog, work Hourglass Pattern as established to M, SSK, K to end. 2 sts dec.
Rnd 2: K to M, work Hourglass Pattern to M, K to end.
Rep Rnds 1–2 another 12 (15, 16) times. 68 (74, 82) sts.

Foot
WE as established until foot measures approx 1.5 (2, 2.25)" shorter than desired length.

Toe
Transition Rnd — Sizes 7.25 (8, -)": K to M, remove M, SSK, K5, (SSK, K6) two times, K2tog, K6, K2tog, K5, K2tog, remove M, K to end. 6 sts dec.
Transition Rnd — Size 8.75": K to M, remove M, (SSK, K5) three times, SSK, K6, (K2tog, K5) three times, K2tog, remove M, K to end. 8 sts dec.

Resume all sizes. 62 (68, 74) sts on needles.
Setup Rnd: K15 (17, 18), PM, K32 (34, 38), PM, K to end.
Rnd 1: K to 2 sts before M, K2tog, SM, K1 (0, 1), SSK, K to 3 (2, 3) sts before M, K2tog, K1 (0, 1), SM, SSK, K to end. 4 sts dec.
Rnd 2: K all.
Rep Rnds 1–2 another 7 (11, 12) times. 30 (20, 22) sts.
Rep Rnd 1 another 3 (0, 0) times. 18 (20, 22) sts.

Break yarn, leaving at least 15" tail.
Graft toe closed using Kitchener Stitch.

Second Sock
Make second sock as first, being sure to work Heel Flap and Heel Gusset correctly, which differ from first sock.

Finishing
Weave in ends, wash, and block as desired.

Cable Pattern

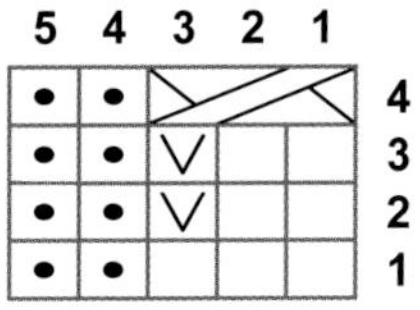

LEGEND

No Stitch
Placeholder—no stitch made

K
RS: Knit stitch
WS: Purl stitch

P
RS: Purl stitch
WS: Knit stitch

Sl
RS: Slip stitch purl-wise, with yarn in back
WS: Slip stitch purl-wise, with yarn in front

Right Twist, Purl back (RPT)
Sl1 to CN, hold in back; K1, P1 from CN

Left Twist, Purl back (LPT)
Sl1 to CN, hold in front; P1, K1 from CN

1 over 2 Right Cable (1/2 RC)
Sl2 to CN, hold in back; K1, K2 from CN

Right Cable Decrease (RCD)
Sl2 to CN, hold in back; K1, K2tog from CN

BOR Marker

Chart 1

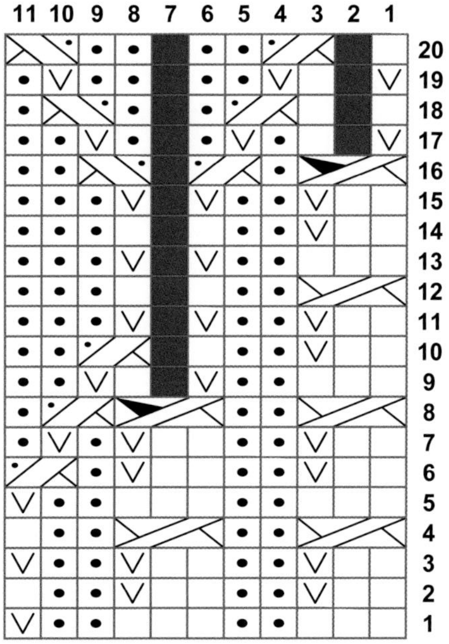

between beginning and center of rnd

Chart 2

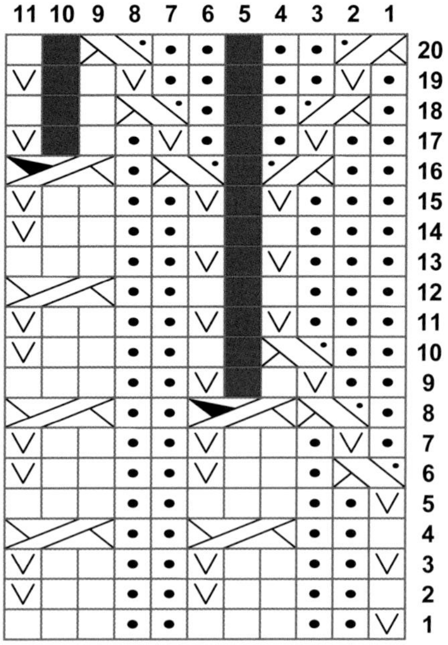

between center and end of rnd

Chart 3, 7.25 (-, 8.75)" sizes

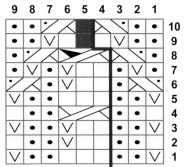

incorporating last cable and moving BOR M

Chart 3, - (8, -)" size

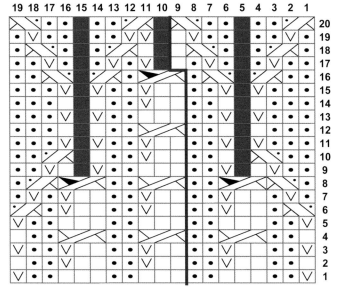

incorporating last cables and moving BOR M

Hourglass Pattern

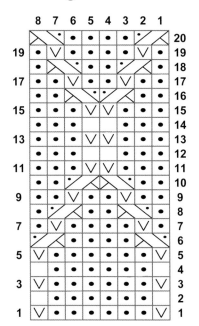

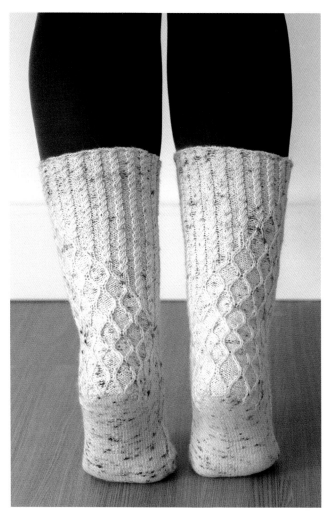

PISTACHIO
by Lauren Rose

FINISHED MEASUREMENTS

7 (8, 9, 10)″ circumference × 8.75 (9.25, 9.5, 10)″ foot length (length is adjustable), to fit US shoe sizes 6.5–7 (7.5–8, 8.5–9, 9.5–10); meant to be worn with approx 10% negative ease

YARN

Muse™ Hand Painted Sock Yarn (fingering weight, 75% Superwash Merino Wool, 25% Nylon; 423 yards/100g): Joyous 28807 or Elation 28153 (seen in tutorials), 1 (1, 2, 2) hanks

NEEDLES

US 1 (2.25mm) DPNs or two circular needles for two circulars technique or 32″ or longer circular needles for Magic Loop technique, or size to obtain gauge

NOTIONS

Yarn Needle
Stitch Markers

GAUGE

32 sts and 50 rnds = 4″ in Stockinette Stitch, blocked

For pattern support, contact lauroftheblings@gmail.com

Pistachio

Notes:

Highly variegated rainbow yarns are so fun to buy, but can be intimidating to knit. Elongated stitches showcase them perfectly—creating a long bright stitch on top of darker ones, or the reverse, is such a delight!

Pistachio socks are knit from the cuff down, with a pattern of elongated stitches that fans out from the center and disappears the same way. After working the eye-of-partridge heel flap, the stitch pattern is repeated again on the foot, ending with a wedge toe.

The Vee stitches will grow outwards from the center of the instep and back of leg. New repeats are offset from previous ones by 2 stitches in either direction. Each 4-row repeat adds one more Vee to the previous repeat. This happens on both instep and back of the leg, until eventually the two expanding patterns meet. Then the Vees start to disappear from the center of the instep/back of leg out. This is accomplished by working only half of each stitch (Vee-R and Vee-L) in the center, expanding in either direction by 2 stitches each repeat.

Vee

Insert RH needle four rnds down between second and third st on LH needle (counting loop on needle as first rnd), and draw up a loop from behind sock through to front. K4, then insert RH needle five rnds down between second and third st on RH needle (same place used for previous loop), and draw up a loop. Do not pull loop tight and compress fabric—keep enough slack in long loop so it lays across top of fabric. Note that right and left "legs" of this st are sometimes referred to as "elongated sts" in pattern.

Vee-L

Insert RH needle five rnds down between second and third st on RH needle, and draw up a loop.

Vee-R

Insert RH needle four rnds down, between second and third stitch on LN, and draw up a loop.

Calf Shaping (optional)

First, measure calf where top of sock will hit and round to the nearest 0.25": _____"

Multiply that number by 8 and round to the nearest even number: _____
This is the CO count.
After working 1x1 Rib with this number of sts, dec to one of the four sizes provided while working the leg.

Depending on target size for the foot, arrange sts as follows: 28 (32, 36, 40) sts on instep, remainder on back of leg.

Calculate how many sts are on back of leg by subtracting instep count provided above from total CO count: _____

Calculate how many sts need to be decreased. Take back of leg count and subtract instep count: _____

Decs are worked in pairs, so take the number above and divide by 2. This is the number of paired decs: _____

After working the ribbing, you'll work decs on leg. (The back of leg decs will coincide with the Vee rnds.)

Where to place the first Vee on back of leg? Divide number of sts on back of leg by 2: _____

Subtract 2 from that number: _____
K that many, work Vee, K to BOR. Subsequent Vees will be placed relative to that first Vee.
Example: 44 sts on back of leg. Divided by 2 = 22, subtract 2 = 20. K20, work Vee, K to end.
Work dec rnds as follows.
Rnd 1: Work instep in pattern; on back of leg, K1, SSK, work instep in pattern to last 3 sts, K2tog, K1.
Rnds 2–4: K all.
Cont working decs as established until target st count is reached.

DIRECTIONS

Cuff

Using German Twisted Cast On or preferred stretchy cast on, CO 56 (64, 72, 80) sts. Join to work in the rnd, being careful not to twist sts. PM for BOR.
Rnd 1: K28 (32, 36, 40) instep sts, PM, K28 (32, 36, 40) back of leg sts to end.

Work 1x1 Rib for twelve rnds.

Leg

Knit four rnds.

Setup Rnd 1: *K12 (14, 16, 18), work Vee once, K to M; rep from * across back of leg.
Setup Rnd 2: *K to first elongated st, SSK, K2, K2tog, K to M; rep from * across back of leg.
Setup Rnds 3–4: K all.

Expanding Vees
For subsequent Vees, insert needle to draw up loop next to where loop from previous Vee st was placed on needle; there will be a natural gap there.
Rnd 1: *K to 2 sts before start of previous Vee, work Vees until 2 sts after end of previous Vees, K to M; rep from * across back of leg.
Rnd 2: *K to first elongated st, (SSK, K2, K2tog) to end of elongated sts, K to M; rep from * across back of leg.
Rnds 3–4: K all.
Rep Rnds 1–4 five more times. Seven Vees each on instep and back of leg.

Disappearing Vees

Size 7 (-, -, -)" Only

Setup Rnd 1: K2, Vee-L, work Vees until 10 K sts have been worked (does not include loops added as part of Vee—this is 4 sts from center of instep), Vee-R, K8, Vee-L, work Vees to end of instep (a Vee will straddle M); work Vees until 10 sts have been worked (including finishing the half-Vee begun on instep), Vee-R, K8, Vee-L, work Vees to last 2 sts, Vee-R, K2.

Setup Rnd 2: K1, K2tog, (SSK, K2, K2tog) to end of full Vees, SSK to process Vee-L, K to 1 before Vee-R, K2tog, (SSK, K2, K2tog) to last 3 sts, SSK, K1.

Rnds 3–4: K all.

Sizes - (8, 9, 10)" Only

These sizes simultaneously cont to add more Vees on outside until they reach edge of instep/back of leg.

Rnd 1: *K to 2 sts before start of previous Vee (Size 8" will already be there—begin working Vees immediately), work Vees until 12 (14, 16) K sts have been worked (does not include loops added as part of Vee—this is 4 sts from center of instep), Vee-R, K8, Vee-L, work Vees to 2 sts after end of previous Vees, K to M; rep from * across back of leg.

Rnd 2: *K to first elongated st, (SSK, K2, K2tog) to end of full Vees, SSK to process Vee-L, K to 1 st before Vee-R, K2tog, (SSK, K2, K2tog) to end of elongated sts, K to M; rep from * across back of leg.

Rnds 3–4: K all.

Sizes - (-, 9, 10)" Only

Rnd 5: *K to 2 sts before start of previous Vee, work Vees to 2 sts before previous Vee-R, Vee-R, K to 2 sts after previous Vee-L, Vee-L, work Vees to 2 sts after end of previous Vees, K to M; rep from * across back of leg.

Rnd 6: *K to first elongated st, (SSK, K2, K2tog) to end of full Vees, SSK to process Vee-L, K to 1 st before Vee-R, K2tog, (SSK, K2, K2tog) to end of elongated sts, K to M; rep from * across back of leg.

Rnds 7–8: K all.

Rep Rnds 5–8 another - (-, 0, 1) time.

Resume All Sizes

To keep Vees offset from each other, there will now be two alternating rep of four rnds. Begin with working Set B (A, A, A), then alternate to Set A (B, B, B) and so on.

Set A

Rnd A1: K2, Vee-L, work Vees to 2 sts before previous Vee-R, Vee-R, K to 2 sts after previous Vee-L, Vee-L, work Vees to end of instep and onto back of leg (a Vee will straddle M) to 2 sts before previous Vee-R, Vee-R, K to 2 sts after previous Vee-L, Vee-L, work Vees to last 2 sts, Vee-R, K2.

Rnd A2: K1, K2tog, (SSK, K2, K2tog) to end of full Vees, SSK to process Vee-L, K to 1 st before Vee-R, K2tog, (SSK, K2, K2tog) to last 3 sts, SSK, K1.

Rnds A3–A4: K all.

Set B

Rnd B1: (Work Vees to 2 sts before previous Vee-R, Vee-R, K to 2 sts after previous Vee-L, Vee-L, work Vees to M) two times.

Rnd B2: (SSK, K2, K2tog) to end of full Vees, SSK to process Vee-L, K to 1 st before Vee-R, K2tog, (SSK, K2, K2tog) to end.

Rnds B3–B4: K all.

Cont alternating Set A and Set B Rnds 1–4 until all full Vees are gone. The final rep is as follows.

Rnd 1: (Vee-R, K to M, Vee-L) two times.

Rnd 2: (SSK, K to 1 st before previous elongated st, K2tog) two times.

Rnds 3–4: K all.

For a longer leg, cont working St st until desired leg length is reached, then cont to heel.

Heel Flap

Heel flap is worked over only the 28 (32, 36, 40) back of leg sts.

Setup Row: Turn to work WS, Sl1 WYIF, P to M.

Row 1 (RS): (Sl1 WYIB, K1) to end of heel sts.
Row 2 (WS): Sl1 WYIF, P to end of heel sts.
Row 3: Sl2 WYIB, (K1, Sl1 WYIB) to last 2 heel sts, K2.
Row 4: Sl1 WYIF, P to end of heel sts.
Rep Rows 1–4 another 7 (8, 9, 10) times, ending after Row 4. 33 (37, 41, 45) total heel rows.

Heel Turn

Short Row 1 (RS): Sl1 WYIB, K16 (18, 20, 22), SSK, K1, turn.
Short Row 2 (WS): Sl1 WYIF, P7, P2tog, P1, turn.
Short Row 3: Sl1 WYIB, K to 1 st before gap, SSK, K1, turn.
Short Row 4: Sl1 WYIF, P to 1 st before gap, P2tog, P1, turn.
Rep Short Rows 3–4 until all heel sts have been worked. 18 (20, 22, 24) sts.

Gusset Setup Row (RS): K to end of heel sts, PU and K 17 (19, 21, 23) sts along edge of heel flap plus 1 st in gap, K across instep sts, PU and K 17 (19, 21, 23) sts along edge of heel flap plus 1 st in gap, K to end. 82 (92, 102, 112) total sts.

Foot

Foot reps same chevron pattern as leg on instep while working gusset decs on sole until original st count is reached. Because Vees are not continued onto sole sts, once Vees reach edge of instep, pattern begins/ends with Vee-R and Vee-L. Work decs as instructed on sole until 28 (32, 36, 40) sts remain for sole; then cont sole sts in St st without decs.

Setup Rnd 1: K12 (14, 16, 18), work Vee once, K to M, SM, K1, SSK, K to last 3 sts, K2tog, K1.
Setup Rnd 2: K to first elongated st, SSK, K2, K2tog, K to end.
Setup Rnd 3: K to M, K1, SSK, K to last 3 sts, K2tog, K1.
Setup Rnd 4: K all.

Expanding Vees

Rnd 1: K to 2 sts before start of previous Vee, work Vees to 2 sts after end of previous Vees, K to M, SM, K1, SSK, K to last 3 sts, K2tog, K1.
Rnd 2: K to first elongated st, (SSK, K2, K2tog) to end of elongated sts, K to end.
Rnd 3: K to M, K1, SSK, K to last 3 st, K2tog, K1.
Rnd 4: K all.
Rep Rnds 1–4, working one more Vee rep each time, five more times. Seven Vees on instep.

Disappearing Vees

Size 7 (-, -, -)" Only

Rnd 1: K2, Vee-L, work Vees until 10 sts have been worked, Vee-R, K8, Vee-L, work Vees to 2 sts before M, Vee-R, K2, SM, K1, SSK, K to last 3 sts, K2tog, K1.

Rnd 2: K1, K2tog, (SSK, K2, K2tog) to end of full Vees, SSK to process Vee-L, K to 1 st before Vee-R, K2tog, (SSK, K2, K2tog) to end of full Vees, SSK, K1, SM. K to end.

Rnd 3: K to M, SM, K1, SSK, K to last 3 sts, K2tog, K1.

Rnd 4: K all.

Sizes - (8, 9, 10)" Only

Similar to leg, in addition to removing Vees from center out, these sizes will simultaneously cont to add more Vees on outside until they reach edge of instep.

Rnd 1: K to 2 sts before start of previous Vee, work Vees until 12 (14, 16) sts have been worked, Vee-R, K8, Vee-L, work Vees to 2 sts after end of previous Vees, K to M, SM, K1, SSK, K to last 3 sts, K2tog, K1.

Rnd 2: K to first elongated st, (SSK, K2, K2tog) to end of full Vees, SSK to process Vee-L, K to 1 st before Vee-R, K2tog, (SSK, K2, K2tog) to end of elongated sts, K to end.

Rnd 3: K to M, K1, SSK, K to last 3 sts, K2tog, K1.

Rnd 4: K all.

Sizes - (-, 9, 10)" Only

Rnd 5: K to 2 sts before start of previous Vee, work Vees to 2 sts before previous Vee-R, Vee-R, K to 2 sts after previous Vee-L, Vee-L, work Vees to 2 sts after end of previous Vees, K to M, SM, K1, SSK, K to last 3 sts, K2tog, K1.

Rnd 6: K to first elongated st, (SSK, K2, K2tog) to end of full Vees, SSK to process Vee-L, K to 1 st before Vee-R, K2tog, (SSK, K2, K2tog) to end of elongated sts, K to end.

Rnd 7: K to M, SM, K1, SSK, K to last 3 sts, K2tog, K1.

Rnd 8: K all.

Rep Rnds 5–8 another - (-, 0, 1) time.

Resume All Sizes

To keep Vees offset from each other, there will now be two alternating reps of four rnds. Begin with working Set B (A, A, A), then alternate to Set A (B, B, B) and so on.

Set A

Rnd A1: K2, Vee-L, work Vees to 2 sts before previous Vee-R, Vee-R, K to 2 sts after previous Vee-L, Vee-L, work Vees to 2 sts before M, Vee-R, K2, SM, K1, SSK, K to last 3 sts, K2tog, K1.

Rnd A2: K1, K2tog, (SSK, K2, K2tog) to end of full Vees, SSK to process Vee-L, K to 1 st before Vee-R, K2tog, (SSK, K2, K2tog) to end of full Vees, SSK, K1, SM, K to end.

Rnd A3: K to M, SM, K1, SSK, K to last 3 sts, K2tog, K1.

Rnd A4: K all.

Set B

Rnd B1: Work Vees to 2 sts before previous Vee-R, Vee-R, K to 2 sts after previous Vee-L, Vee-L, work Vees to M, SM, K1, SSK, K to last 3 sts, K2tog, K1.

Rnd B2: (SSK, K2, K2tog) to end of full Vees, SSK to process Vee-L, K to 1 st before Vee-R, K2tog, (SSK, K2, K2tog) to M, SM, K to end.

Rnd B3: K to M, SM, K1, SSK, K to last 3 sts, K2tog, K1.

Rnd B4: K all.

Cont alternating Set A and Set B until all full Vees are gone. Once sole is back to 28 (32, 36, 40) sts, knit all sole sts; no more gusset decs are worked. The final rep will be as follows.

Rnd 1: Vee-R, K to M, Vee-L, SM, K to end.

Rnd 2: SSK, K to 1 st before previous elongated st, K2tog, SM, K to end.

Rnds 3–4: K all.

Work St st on instep and sole until sock measures 1.25 (1.5, 1.5, 1.75)" shorter than desired length.

Toe

Rnd 1: (K1, SSK, K to 3 sts before M, K2tog, K1, SM) two times. 4 sts dec.

Rnd 2: K all.

Rep Rnds 1–2 another 5 (5, 5, 7) times. 16 (20, 24, 24) sts each on instep and sole; 32 (40, 48, 48) sts total.

Rep Rnd 1 another 4 (5, 6, 6) times. 8 (10, 12, 12) sts each on instep and sole; 16 (20, 24, 24) sts total.

Use Kitchener Stitch or preferred grafting method to graft remaining sts tog.

Second Sock

Make second sock same as the first.

Finishing

Weave in ends, wash, and gently block.

1. Insert RH needle 4 rnds down between second and third st on LH needle

2. K to 2 before start of previous Vee

3. Work Vees until 2 sts after end of previous Vees

4. Work Vees until 4 sts from center of instep

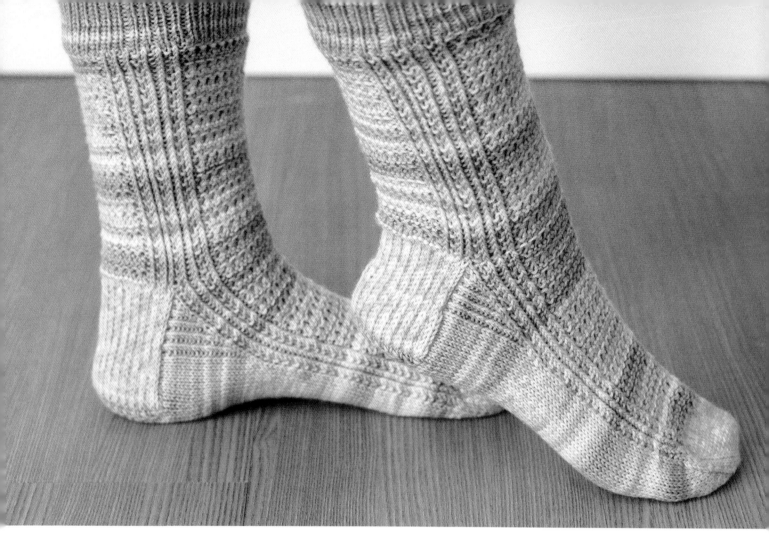

SPARKLING CRYSTALS
by Aud Bergo

FINISHED MEASUREMENTS

6.25 (7, 7.75, 8.5)" leg circumference ×
8.75 (9, 9.25, 9.75)" foot length, to fit
US shoe sizes 7 (7.5–8, 8.5–9, 9.5–10);
meant to be worn with approx 10%
negative ease

YARN

Static™ (fingering weight, 75% Superwash
Wool, 25% Nylon; 437 yards/100g):
Peachy 28493, 1 (1, 1, 1) hank

NEEDLES

US 2 (2.75mm) 32" circular needles for
Magic Loop technique or DPNs or two
24" for two circulars technique, or size
to obtain gauge

US 1 (2.25mm) 32" circular needles for
Magic Loop technique or DPNs or two
24" for two circulars technique, or one
size smaller than size used to obtain
gauge

NOTIONS

Yarn Needle
Stitch Marker

GAUGE

40 sts and 40 rnds = 4" in Texture
Pattern in the round, relaxed, unblocked
32 sts and 44 rnds = 4" in Stockinette
Stitch in the round, unblocked

For pattern support, contact audbergo@hotmail.com

Sparkling Crystals

Notes:

Imagine crystals sparkling in the sunshine. The knit/purl texture pattern for these socks creates the illusion of tiny crystals. They are the perfect showcase for Static yarn, as the varying color stripes mimic sparkling crystals on a lovely sunny day.

Sparkling Crystals Socks are worked top down with an easy-to-memorize texture pattern. They have a slipped stitch heel flap and a twisted ribbed gusset. The sole is knit in Stockinette Stitch.

Leg length is adjustable. For a shorter or longer leg, adjust number of pattern repeats, but end on the round number specified in the directions.

A smaller needle size is used for cuff, heel, and toe. This gives more strength to heel and toe, and a bit tighter cuff to help socks stay in place around the leg.

Instructions are given for Magic Loop or the two circular needle technique, but can be easily adjusted to DPNs by dividing stitches on each needle between two DPNs.

All rounds begin with front of leg/instep (Needle 1), followed by back of leg/gusset/sole (Needle 2).

Charts are worked in the round; read each chart row from right to left as a RS row.

To make two identical socks, take care of the following.
Winding up yarn hank: Start winding the yarn from the outer edge. Knitting the first sock then starts from the inner yarn end. Stripes as shown on photographed socks will then emerge from the cuff onwards.
Before ending first sock: Watch for when yarn stripe repeat ends and a new repeat starts. If a new repeat starts when working the toe, the yarn can be cut and first sock put aside. Use the new repeat to start working on the second sock and go back and finish the first sock after the second sock is finished. On the photographed socks in Size 7.75", a new striping repeat started just after the first sock was finished. Alternatively, just work with the yarn and let the striping yarn pattern create a unique pair of socks.

Leg Back — Size 6.25" (in the round over 30 sts)
Rnd 1: K1 TBL, K1, K1 TBL, P1, K22, P1, K1 TBL, K1, K1 TBL.
Rnd 2: (K1 TBL, P1) two times, (P2tog) eleven times, (P1, K1 TBL) two times.
Rnd 3: K1 TBL, K1, K1 TBL, P1, (KFB) eleven times, P1, K1 TBL, K1, K1 TBL.
Rnd 4: (K1 TBL, P1) two times, P22, (P1, K1 TBL) two times.
Rep Rnds 1–4 for pattern.

Leg Front & Instep — Size 6.25" (in the round over 32 sts)
Rnd 1: P1, K1 TBL, K1, K1 TBL, P1, K22, P1, K1 TBL, K1, K1 TBL, P1.
Rnd 2: P1, (K1 TBL, P1) two times, (P2tog) eleven times, (P1, K1 TBL) two times, P1.

Rnd 3: P1, K1 TBL, K1, K1 TBL, P1, (KFB) eleven times, P1, K1 TBL, K1, K1 TBL, P1.
Rnd 4: (P1, K1 TBL) two times, P24, (K1 TBL, P1) two times.
Rep Rnds 1–4 for pattern.

Leg Back — Sizes - (7, 7.75, 8.5)" (in the round over - (34, 38, 42) sts)
Rnd 1: K1 TBL, P1, K1 TBL, K1, K1 TBL, P1, K- (22, 26, 30), P1, K1 TBL, K1, K1 TBL, P1, K1 TBL.
Rnd 2: (K1 TBL, P1) three times, (P2tog) 11 (13, 15) times, (P1, K1 TBL) three times.
Rnd 3: K1 TBL, P1, K1 TBL, K1, K1 TBL, P1, (KFB) 11 (13, 15) times, P1, K1 TBL, K1, K1 TBL, P1, K1 TBL.
Rnd 4: (K1 TBL, P1) three times, P- (22, 26, 30), (P1, K1 TBL) three times.
Rep Rnds 1–4 for pattern.

Leg Front & Instep — Sizes - (7, 7.75, 8.5)" (in the round over - (36, 40, 44) sts)
Rnd 1: K1, K1 TBL, P1, K1 TBL, K1, K1 TBL, P1, K- (22, 26, 30), P1, K1 TBL, K1, K1 TBL, P1, K1 TBL, K1.
Rnd 2: P1, (K1 TBL, P1) three times, (P2tog) 11 (13, 15) times, (P1, K1 TBL) three times, P1.
Rnd 3: K1, K1 TBL, P1, K1 TBL, K1, K1 TBL, P1, (KFB) 11 (13, 15) times, P1, K1 TBL, K1, K1 TBL, P1, K1 TBL, K1.
Rnd 4: (P1, K1 TBL) three times, P- (24, 28, 32), (K1 TBL, P1) three times.
Rep Rnds 1–4 for pattern.

DIRECTIONS

Cuff
Using smaller needles, CO 62 (70, 78, 86) sts.
Turn and work 1x1 Rib while distributing sts as follows: Leg Front, Needle 1—32 (36, 40, 44) sts; Leg Back, Needle 2—30 (34, 38, 42) sts.
Join to work in the rnd, being careful not to twist sts; PM for BOR.
Work 1x1 Rib for 17 rnds. Piece measures approx 1.5".

Leg
Change to larger needles.
Rnds 1–4: Needle 1—work Leg Front & Instep from chart or written instructions; Needle 2—work Leg Back from chart or written instructions.
Rep Rnds 1–4 another 11 (11, 11, 13) times. Remove M.

Heel Flap
The heel flap is worked back and forth on Needle 2 over 30 (34, 38, 42) sts. Change to smaller needles. Turn work to start on WS.
Row 1 (WS): Sl1 WYIF, P to end.
Row 2 (RS): (Sl1 WYIB, K1) to end.
Rep Rows 1–2 another 17 (19, 19, 21) times. Flap measures approx 2.25 (2.5, 2.5, 2.75)".

Heel Turn

Short Row 1 (WS): Sl1 WYIF, P16 (18, 20, 22), P2tog, P1, turn. 1 st dec.

Short Row 2 (RS): Sl1 WYIB, K5, SSK, K1, turn. 1 st dec.

Short Row 3: Sl1 WYIF, P to 1 st before gap, P2tog, P1, turn. 1 st dec.

Short Row 4: Sl1 WYIB, K to 1 st before gap, SSK, K1, turn. 1 st dec.

Rep Short Rows 3–4 until all sts before gaps are worked. 18 (20, 22, 24) heel sts.

Gusset

The gusset is formed by picking up sts on each side of heel flap and working across sole sts. Change to larger needles.

Left Gusset Setup Partial Rnd: With RS facing, PU and K 16 (17, 18, 20) sts along left side of heel flap, PM for BOR and resume working in the rnd.

Right Gusset Setup Rnd: Needle 1—work Rnd 1 of Leg Front & Instep; Needle 2—PU and K 16 (17, 18, 20) sts along right side of heel flap, K18 (20, 22, 24) heel sts, K6 (7, 8, 8), (P1, K1 TBL) 4 (4, 4, 5) times, P1, K1. 32 (36, 40, 44) sts on Needle 1, 50 (54, 58, 64) sts on Needle 2; 82 (90, 98, 108) sts total.

Gusset Shaping

The gusset is shaped by working decreases on Needle 2.

Needle 1

All Rnds: Cont as established from Leg Front & Instep, starting with pattern Rnd 2.

Needle 2

Rnd 1: K1, (P1, K1 TBL) 4 (4, 4, 5) times, P1, K30 (34, 38, 42), (P1, K1 TBL) 4 (4, 4, 5) times, P1, K1.

Rnd 2: SSK, (K1 TBL, P1) 4 (4, 4, 5) times, K30 (34, 38, 42), (P1, K1 TBL) 4 (4, 4, 5) times K2tog. 2 sts dec.

Rnd 3 and all odd-numbered rnds: Work sts same as shown from previous rnd (K or K TBL the knit sts and P the purl sts).

Rnd 4: SSK, (P1, K1 TBL) 3 (3, 3, 4) times, P1, K30 (34, 38, 42), (P1, K1 TBL) 3 (3, 3, 4) times, P1, K2tog. 2 sts dec.

Rnd 6: SSK, (K1 TBL, P1) 3 (3, 3, 4) times, K30 (34, 38, 42), (P1, K1 TBL) 3 (3, 3, 4) times, K2tog. 2 sts dec.

Rnd 8: SSK, (P1, K1 TBL) 2 (2, 2, 3) times, P1, K30 (34, 38, 42), (P1, K1 TBL) 2 (2, 2, 3) times, P1, K2tog. 2 sts dec.

Rnd 10: SSK, (K1 TBL, P1) 2 (2, 2, 3) times, K30 (34, 38, 42), (P1, K1 TBL) 2 (2, 2, 3) times, K2tog. 2 sts dec.

Rnd 12: SSK, (P1, K1 TBL) 1 (1, 1, 2) times, P1, K30 (34, 38, 42), (P1, K1 TBL) 1 (1, 1, 2) times, P1, K2tog. 2 sts dec.

Rnd 14: SSK, (K1 TBL, P1) 1 (1, 1, 2) times, K30 (34, 38, 42), (P1, K1 TBL) 1 (1, 1, 2) times K2tog. 2 sts dec.

Sizes 6.25 (7, 7.75, -)" Only

Rnd 16: SSK, P1, K to last 3 sts, P1, K2tog. 2 sts dec.

Rnd 18: SSK, K to last 2 sts, K2tog. 2 sts dec.

Rnds 20 and 22: Rep Rnd 18. 28 (32, 36) sts.

Size 8.5" Only

Rnd 16: SSK, P1, K1 TBL, P1, K to last 5 sts, P1, K1 TBL, P1, K2tog. 2 sts dec.

Rnd 18: SSK, K1 TBL, P1, K to last 4 sts, P1, K1 TBL, K2tog. 2 sts dec.

Rnd 20: SSK, P1, K to last 3 sts, P1, K2tog. 2 sts dec.

Rnd 22: SSK, K to last 2 sts, K2tog. 2 sts dec.

Rnd 24: Rep Rnd 22. 40 sts.

Foot (resume all sizes)

Cont working sole in St st and instep pattern as established until foot measures 1.5 (1.75, 2, 2.25)" shorter than desired length, measured from back of heel to live sts. End on pattern Rnd 3. If additional length is needed, knit one, two, or three additional rnds.

Toe

Change to smaller needles. When working toe, sts should be equally divided between Needle 1 and 2. For all sizes, move first and last sts from instep to sole; 30 (34, 38, 42) sts on each needle. Move M for BOR.

Rnd 1: K all.

Rnd 2: Needle 1—K1, SSK, K to last 3 sts, K2tog, K1; Needle 2—work same as for Needle 1. 2 sts dec each needle; 4 sts dec total.

Rep Rnds 1–2 four more times. 40 (48, 56, 64) sts. Work Rnd 2 until 12 sts remain in total.

Break yarn, leaving a 15" tail. With tail threaded onto a yarn needle, graft sts closed using Kitchener Stitch. Alternatively, thread tail through sts, pulling tight to close hole. Fasten off.

Second Sock

Make second sock from same directions as first. If an identical second sock is wanted, see comments about color repeats under *Notes*.

Finishing

Weave in ends, wash, and block as desired.

Leg Back, 6.25″ size

10	9	8	7	6	5	4	3	2	1	
Ω	•	Ω	•	•	•	•	Ω	•	Ω	4
Ω	•	Ω	•	■	KFB	•	Ω	•	Ω	3
Ω	•	Ω	•	■	P2tog	•	Ω	•	Ω	2
Ω		Ω					Ω		Ω	1

work rep sts 11 times

Leg Back, - (7, 7.75, 8.5)″ size

14	13	12	11	10	9	8	7	6	5	4	3	2	1	
Ω	•	Ω	•	Ω	•	•	•	•	Ω	•	Ω	•	Ω	4
Ω	•	Ω	•	Ω	•	■	KFB	•	Ω	•	Ω	•	Ω	3
Ω	•	Ω	•	Ω	•	■	P2tog	•	Ω	•	Ω	•	Ω	2
Ω	•	Ω	•	Ω	•			•	Ω	•	Ω	•	Ω	1

work rep sts - (11, 13, 15) times

Leg Front & Instep, 6.25″ size

12	11	10	9	8	7	6	5	4	3	2	1	
•	Ω	•	Ω	•	•	•	•	Ω	•	Ω	•	4
•	Ω	•	Ω	•	■	KFB	•	Ω	•	Ω	•	3
•	Ω	•	Ω	•	■	P2tog	•	Ω	•	Ω	•	2
•	Ω	•	Ω	•			•	Ω	•	Ω	•	1

work rep sts 11 times

Leg Front & Instep, - (7, 7.75, 8.5)″ size

16	15	14	13	12	11	10	9	8	7	6	5	4	3	2	1	
•	Ω	•	Ω	•	Ω	•	•	•	•	Ω	•	Ω	•	Ω	•	4
•	Ω	•	Ω	•	Ω	•	■	KFB	•	Ω	•	Ω	•	Ω	•	3
•	Ω	•	Ω	•	Ω	•	■	P2tog	•	Ω	•	Ω	•	Ω	•	2
•	Ω	•	Ω	•	Ω	•			•	Ω	•	Ω	•	Ω	•	1

work rep sts - (11, 13, 15) times

LEGEND

- ■ **No Stitch** — Placeholder—no stitch made
- ☐ **Knit Stitch**
- • **Purl Stitch**
- Ω **K TBL** — Knit stitch through the back loop
- KFB **KFB** — Knit into the front and back of the stitch
- P2tog **P2tog** — Purl 2 stitches together as one stitch
- ☐ **Pattern Repeat**

THREE STEPS FORWARD
by Paula Niskasaari

FINISHED MEASUREMENTS
6.75 (7.75, 8.75)" foot circumference ×
8.5 (8.75, 9)" foot length, to fit US shoe
sizes 6 (7.5, 9); meant to be worn with
approx 10% negative ease

YARN
Muse™ Hand Painted Sock (fingering
weight, 75% Superwash Merino Wool,
25% Nylon; 423 yards/100g): Hope
Speckle 28803, 1 hank

NEEDLES
US 1.5 (2.5mm) DPNs or two circular
needles for two circulars technique or
32" or longer circular needles for Magic
Loop technique, or size to obtain gauge

NOTIONS
Yarn Needle
Stitch Markers
Cable Needle

GAUGE
33 sts and 44 rnds = 4" in Stockinette
Stitch in the round, blocked
38 sts and 43 rnds = 4" in Leg Triangle
Stitch in the round, blocked
40 sts and 50 rnds = 4" in Toe Triangle
Stitch in the round, blocked

For pattern support, contact paula@neulovilla.fi

Three Steps Forward

Notes:

Three Steps Forward is a pattern for those gorgeous skeins of hand-painted yarn that are fun to buy, but hard to find good patterns for! It's simple yet interesting to knit and it shows the best of highly variegated yarn.

Three Steps Forward Socks are worked from the cuff down, with a flap heel, and the last stitches in the toe are grafted together using Kitchener Stitch. There are two different cable stitch patterns, which both use slipped stitches and 1/1-cables.

Charts are worked both in the round and flat. When working chart in the round, read each chart row from right to left as a RS row; when working chart flat, read RS rows (even numbers) from right to left, and WS rows (odd numbers) from left to right.

Left Twist Slip (LT-S)
Sl1 to CN, hold in front, K1, Sl1 from CN.

Right Twist Slip (RT-S)
Sl1 to CN, hold in back, Sl1, K1 from CN.

1x1 Twisted Rib
All Rnds: (P1, K1 TBL) to end.

Leg Triangle Stitch (in the round over 13 sts)
Rnd 1 and all odd-numbered rnds: K all.
Rnd 2: (LT-S, K2) three times, K1.
Rnd 4: K1, (LT-S, K2) two times, LT-S, K2.
Rnd 6: (K2, LT-S) three times, K1.
Rnd 8: K1, (K2, LT-S) three times.
Rnd 10: K1, (K2, RT-S) three times.
Rnd 12: (K2, RT-S) three times, K1.
Rnd 14: K1, (RT-S, K2) three times.
Rnd 16: (RT-S, K2) three times, K1.
Rep Rnds 1–16 for pattern.

Leg Triangle Stitch (flat over 13 sts)
Row 1 and all odd-numbered rows: P all.
Row 2: (LT-S, K2) three times, K1.
Row 4: K1, (LT-S, K2) two times, LT-S, K2.
Row 6: (K2, LT-S) three times, K1.
Row 8: K3, (LT-S, K2) two times, LT-S.
Row 10: K1, (K2, RT-S) three times.
Row 12: (K2, RT-S) three times, K1.
Row 14: K1, (RT-S, K2) three times.
Row 16: (RT-S, K2) three times, K1.
Rep Rows 1–16 for pattern.

Toe Triangle Stitch (in the round over a multiple of 10 sts)
Rnd 1: LT-S, K6, RT-S.
Rnd 2 and all even-numbered rnds: K all.
Rnd 3: K1, LT-S, K4, RT-S, K1.
Rnd 5: K2, LT-S, K2, RT-S, K2.
Rnd 7: LT-S, K1, LT-S, RT-S, K1, RT-S.
Rnds 9–14: Rep Rnds 3–8.
Rnds 15–18: Rep Rnds 3–6.
Rnd 19: K3, LT-S, RT-S, K3.

DIRECTIONS

Left Sock
Cuff & Leg
CO 56 (64, 72) sts using Long Tail Cast On. Join to work in the rnd, being careful not to twist sts, PM for BOR.
Work 1x1 Twisted Rib until piece measures 1″ from CO edge.
Next Rnd: K3, work Rnd 1 of Leg Triangle Stitch from chart or written instructions, K to end.

*Cont working St st and pattern st as established, until piece measures 6″ from CO edge, ending after Rnd 3 (1, 15) of pattern.

Heel Flap
Work back and forth on only the first 28 (32, 36) sts for this section.
Row 1 (RS): Sl1 WYIB, K2, work Leg Triangle Stitch as established but flat, K to end, turn.
Row 2 (WS): Sl1 WYIF, P to end, turn.
Rep Rows 1–2 another 12 (14, 16) times.
Next Row (RS): Sl1 WYIB, K to end.
Next Row (WS): Sl1 WYIF, P to end. 14 (16, 18) slipped sts on each side of heel flap.

Heel Turn
Setup Row (RS): Sl1 WYIB, K17 (20, 22), SSK, turn. 1 st dec.
Short Row 1 (WS): Sl1 WYIF, P8 (10, 10), P2tog, turn. 1 st dec.
Short Row 2: Sl1 WYIB, K8 (10, 10), SSK, turn. 1 st dec.
Rep Short Rows 1–2 another 7 (8, 10) times and then Row 1 once more. There are 10 (12, 12) heel sts left.
Next Row (RS): Sl1 WYIB, K4 (5, 5).

Gusset
PM to indicate new BOR. Resume working in the rnd.
Setup Rnd: K5 (6, 6), then PU and K 14 (16, 18) sts along heel flap, M1L, PM, K28 (32, 36) across instep sts, PM, M1L, PU and K 14 (16, 18) sts along heel flap, K to end. 68 (78) 86 sts.
Rnd 1: K1 to last 2 sts before M, K2tog, SM, K to M, SM, SSK, K to end. 2 sts dec.
Rnd 2: K all.
Rep Rnds 1–2 another 5 (6, 6) times. 56 (64, 72) sts total.

Foot
Work St st until total foot length is 4.5 (4.75, 5)″, measuring from back of heel to live sts.
Next Rnd: K to M, SM, K4 (1, 3), work Rnd 1 of Toe Triangle Stitch from chart or written instructions 2 (3, 3) times, K to end.
Cont as established, until Toe Triangle Stitch has been completed once in full.
Work St st until total foot length is 6.5 (6.5, 7.5)″ or 1.75 (2, 2.25)″ shorter than desired length.

Toe

Rnd 1: (K to 3 sts before M, K2tog, K1, SM, K1, SSK) two times, K to end. 4 sts dec.

Rnd 2: K all.

Rep Rnds 1–2 another 6 (7, 8) times until 28 (32, 36) sts remain in total.

Rep Rnd 1 another 4 (5, 6) times. 12 sts remain.

End Toe: K3. Break yarn, leaving a 12" tail.

If using DPNs, place instep sts on one needle and heel sts on another.

Graft instep and heel sts tog using Kitchener Stitch.

Right Sock

Cuff & Leg

CO 56 (64, 72) sts using Long Tail Cast On. Join to work in the rnd, being careful not to twist sts, PM for BOR.

Work 1x1 Twisted Rib until piece measures 1" from CO edge.

Next Rnd: K13 (17, 21), work Rnd 1 of Leg Triangle Stitch from chart or written instructions, K to end.

Work the rest of right sock same as left from * to end, with stitch pattern as established.

Finishing

Weave in ends, wash, and block as desired.

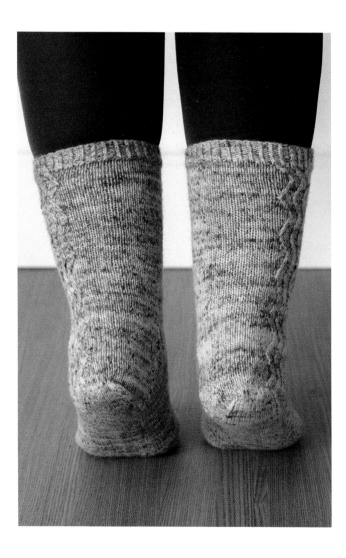

Leg Triangle Stitch

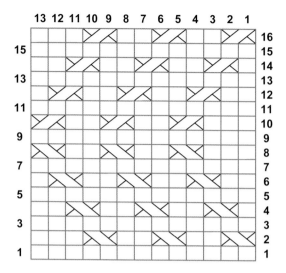

Toe Triangle Stitch

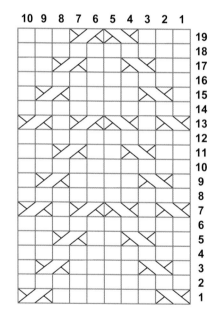

LEGEND

☐ Knit Stitch

Right Twist Slip (RT-S)
Sl1 to CN, hold in back; Sl1, K1 from CN

Left Twist Slip (LT-S)
Sl1 to CN, hold in front; K1, Sl1 from CN

TOPAZ
by Nancy Vandivert

FINISHED MEASUREMENTS

7.5 (8, 8.5, 8.75, 9.25, 10.25)" leg circumference × 8.75 (8.75, 8.75 9.5, 9.75, 10)" foot length, to fit US shoe sizes 6 (8–8.5, 9.5–10); meant to be worn with approx 10% negative ease

YARN

Hawthorne™ (fingering weight, 80% Fine Superwash Highland Wool, 20% Polyamide (Nylon); 357 yards/100g): Cattail Kettle 28620, 1 (1, 2, 2, 2, 2) hank(s)

NEEDLES

US 1.5 (2.5mm) DPNs or two circular needles for two circulars technique or 32" or longer circular needles for Magic Loop technique, or size to obtain gauge

NOTIONS

Yarn Needle
Stitch Markers

GAUGE

35 sts and 52 rnds = 4" in Size 7.25" Pattern, lightly blocked

For pattern support, contact ngvandivert@gmail.com

Topaz

Notes:

When polished, topaz reveals its mysterious nature: colorful, layered, and softly lustrous, all of which are reflected in the changing textures flowing the length of this sock.

Topaz uses simple increases, decreases, and texture changes. Worked top down with a heel flap and round toe, the width of the basic motif changes between sizes.

Charts are worked in the round; read each chart row from right to left as a RS row.

Ribbing — Size 7.25" (in the round over a multiple of 11 sts)
Rnd 1: (K2 TBL, P2, K3 TBL, P2, K2 TBL) to end.
Rep Rnd 1 for ribbing pattern.

Ribbing — Size 8" (in the round over a multiple of 35 sts)
Rnd 1: (K2 TBL, P2, K3 TBL, P2, K4 TBL, P3, K3 TBL, P3, K4 TBL, P2, K3 TBL, P2, K2 TBL) to end.
Rep Rnd 1 for ribbing pattern.

Ribbing — Size 8.5" (in the round over a multiple of 37 sts)
Rnd 1: (K2 TBL, P3, K3 TBL, P3, K4 TBL, P2, K3 TBL, P2, K4 TBL, P3, K3 TBL, P3, K2 TBL) to end.
Rep Rnd 1 for ribbing pattern.

Ribbing — Size 8.75" (in the round over a multiple of 13 sts)
Rnd 1: (K2 TBL, P3, K3 TBL, P3, K2 TBL) to end.
Rep Rnd 1 for ribbing pattern.

Ribbing — Size 9.25" (in the round over a multiple of 41 sts)
Rnd 1: (K2 TBL, P3, K3 TBL, P3, K4 TBL, P1, K2 TBL, P1, K3 TBL, P1, K2 TBL, P1, K4 TBL, P3, K3 TBL, P3, K2 TBL) to end.
Rep Rnd 1 for ribbing pattern.

Ribbing — Size 10.25" (in the round over a multiple of 15 sts)
Rnd 1: (K2 TBL, P1, K2 TBL, P1, K3 TBL, P1, K2 TBL, P1, K2 TBL) to end.
Rep Rnd 1 for ribbing pattern.

Stitch Pattern — Size 7.25" (in the round over a multiple of 11 sts)
Rnd 1: K2tog, K3, (K1, YO, K1) in 1 st, K3, SSK.
Rnd 2 and all even-numbered Rnds: K all.
Rnd 3: Rep Rnd 1.
Rnd 5: Rep Rnd 1.
Rnd 7: Rep Rnd 1.
Rnd 9: P all.
Rnd 11: P all.
Rep Rnds 1–12 for pattern.

Stitch Pattern — Size 8" (in the round over a multiple of 35 sts)
Rnd 1: K2tog, K3, (K1, YO, K1) in 1 st, K3, SSK, K2tog, K4, (K1, YO, K1) in 1 st, K4, SSK, K2tog, K3, (K1, YO, K1) in 1 st, K3, SSK.
Rnd 2 and all even-numbered Rnds: K all.
Rnd 3: Rep Rnd 1.
Rnd 5: Rep Rnd 1.
Rnd 7: Rep Rnd 1.
Rnd 9: P all.
Rnd 11: P all.
Rep Rnds 1–12 for pattern.

Stitch Pattern — Size 8.5" (in the round over a multiple of 37 sts)
Rnd 1: K2tog, K4, (K1, YO, K1) in 1 st, K4, SSK, K2tog, K3, (K1, YO, K1) in 1 st, K3, SSK, K2tog, K4, (K1, YO, K1) in 1 st, K4, SSK.
Rnd 2 and all even-numbered Rnds: K all.
Rnd 3: Rep Rnd 1.
Rnd 5: Rep Rnd 1.
Rnd 7: Rep Rnd 1.
Rnd 9: P all.
Rnd 11: P all.
Rep Rnds 1–12 for pattern.

Stitch Pattern — Size 8.75" (in the round over a multiple of 13 sts)
Rnd 1: K2tog, K4, (K1, YO, K1) in 1 st, K4, SSK.
Rnd 2: K all.
Rnds 3–8: Rep Rnds 1–2.
Rnd 9: P all.
Rnd 10: K11, P1, K1.
Rnd 11: P all.
Rnd 12: K all.
Rep Rnds 1–12 for pattern.

Stitch Pattern — Size 9.25" (in the round over a multiple of 41 sts)
Rnd 1: K2tog, K4, (K1, YO, K1) in 1 st, K4, SSK, K2tog, K5, (K1, YO, K1) in 1 st, K5, SSK, K2tog, K4, (K1, YO, K1) in 1 st, K4, SSK.
Rnd 2 and all even-numbered Rnds: K all.
Rnd 3: Rep Rnd 1.
Rnd 5: Rep Rnd 1.
Rnd 7: Rep Rnd 1.
Rnd 9: P all.
Rnd 11: P all.
Rep Rnds 1–12 for pattern.

Stitch Pattern — Size 10.25" (in the round over a multiple of 15 sts)
Rnd 1: K2tog, K5, (K1, YO, K1) in 1 st, K5, SSK.
Rnd 2 and all even-numbered Rnds: K all.
Rnd 3: Rep Rnd 1.
Rnd 5: Rep Rnd 1.
Rnd 7: Rep Rnd 1.
Rnd 9: P all.
Rnd 11: P all.
Rep Rnds 1–12 for pattern.

DIRECTIONS

Cuff

Loosely CO 66 (70, 74, 78, 82, 90) sts and join for working in the rnd, being careful not to twist sts. PM for BOR.
Begin Ribbing pattern for selected size and work ribbing for 10 rnds or to desired length.
Next Rnd: K all.

Leg

Begin Stitch Pattern for selected size from chart or written instructions and work pattern six times, or to desired length, ending last rnd with Rnd 11. If helpful, PM between st pattern reps to ensure pattern alignment.

Heel

Setup Row 1 (RS): K2tog, K31 (33, 35, 37, 39, 43), turn work.
Setup Row 2 (WS): P32 (34, 36, 38, 40, 44) heel sts onto one needle. Place remaining 33 (35, 37, 39, 41, 45) sts on spare needle or scrap yarn to work later for top of foot; heel is worked flat across those just-purled sts.

Heel Flap

Row 1 (RS): (Sl1 WYIB, K1) to end.
Row 2 (WS): Sl1 WYIF, P to end.
Row 3: Sl1 WYIB, K2, (Sl1 WYIB, K1) to last st, K1.
Row 4: Sl1 WYIF, P to end.
Rep Rows 1–4 seven more times, or to desired flap length, ending with a WS row.

Heel Turn

Short Row 1 (RS): K18 (19, 20, 21, 22, 23), SSK, K1, turn.
Short Row 2 (WS): Sl1 WYIF, P5, P2tog, P1, turn.
Short Row 3: Sl1 WYIB, K to 1 st before gap made on previous row, SSK (1 st from each side of gap), K1, turn. 1 st dec.
Short Row 4: Sl1 WYIF, P to 1 st before gap made on previous row, P2tog (1 st from each side of gap), P1, turn. 1 st dec.
Rep Short Rows 3–4 until all heel sts have been worked, ending after a WS row and ending the last rep as SSK on Row 3 and P2tog on Row 4 if there are not enough sts to work the final K1 or P1 after the final dec. 18 (19, 20, 21, 22, 23) heel sts.

Gusset

Resume working in the rnd. BOR M should be in middle of heel. If needed, return saved sts to needle.
Setup Rnd: K9 (10, 10, 10, 11, 12), PM for new BOR, K to end of heel turn, PU and K 1 st for each slipped st along edge of heel flap, PM, PU and K 1 st in gap between heel flap and top of foot; begin Rnd 12 of Stitch Pattern for selected size and work across 33 (35, 37, 39, 41, 45) sts, PU and K 1 st in gap between heel flap and top of foot, PM, PU and K 1 st for each slipped st along other edge of heel flap, K to BOR M.
Rnd 1: K to 2 sts before M, K2tog, SM, P1, work next rnd of Stitch Pattern to 1 st before next M, P1, SM, SSK, K to end. 2 sts dec.
Row 2: K to M, SM, P1, work next rnd of Stitch Pattern to 1 st before next M, P1, SM, K to end.
Rep Rnds 1–2 until 65 (69, 73, 77, 81, 89) sts remain, or to desired circumference around foot.

Foot

Cont in pattern as established, working Stitch Pattern on top of foot, keeping 1 P st in between top of foot and St st on bottom of foot, until sock is 2″ shorter than desired length, ending with Rnd 12. If unable to complete a full rep to achieve this length, work several rnds of St st after last full rep until foot is 2″ shorter than desired length.

Toe

Toe is worked in St st over 22 (25, 25, 28, 31, 34) rnds — 1.75 (2, 2, 2.25, 2.5, 2.5)″.
Setup Rnd: *K11 (12, 12, 13, 14, 15), PM; rep from * four more times, K10 (9, 13, 12, 11, 14) to end (BOR M).
Rnd 1: (K to 2 sts before M, K2tog, SM) 5 (5, 6, 5, 5, 5) times, K10 (9, 0, 12, 11, 14) to end. 60 (64, 67, 72, 76, 84) sts.
Rnds 2–3: K all.
Rnd 4: (K to 2 sts before M, K2tog, SM) 6 (5, 6, 6, 5, 6) times, K0 (9, 0, 0, 11, 0) to end. 54 (59, 61, 66, 71, 78) sts.
Rnds 5–6: K all.
Rnd 7: Rep Rnd 4. 48 (54, 55, 60, 66, 72) sts.
Rnds 8–9: K all.
Rnd 10: (K to 2 sts before M, K2tog, SM) six times. 6 sts dec.
Rep Rnds 8–10 another 4 (5, 5, 6, 7, 8) times. 18 (18, 19, 18, 18, 18) sts.

Size - (-, 8.5, -, -, -)″ Only
Next Rnd: K to 2 sts before M, K2tog, SM, K to end. 18 sts.

Arrange remaining sts onto two needles and graft toe closed with Kitchener Stitch.

Second Sock

Make second sock same as first.

Finishing

Weave in ends, wash, and block as desired.

LEGEND

☐	**Knit Stitch**
⊡	**Purl Stitch**
▱	**K2tog** Knit 2 stitches together as one stitch
◺	**SSK** Slip, slip, knit slipped stitches together
▽	**K-YO-K** (Knit 1, Yarn Over, Knit 1) into 1 stitch

Stitch Pattern
Size 7.5 (-, -, -, -, -)"

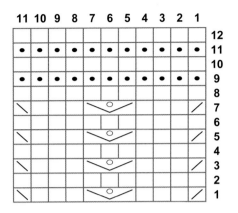

Stitch Pattern
Size - (8, -, -, -, -)"

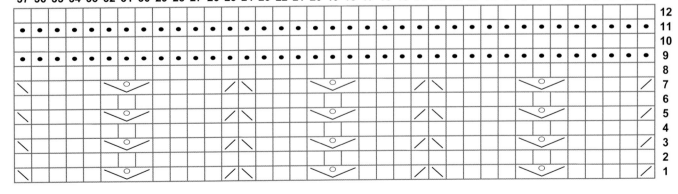

Stitch Pattern
Size - (-, 8.5, -, -, -)"

Stitch Pattern
Size - (-, -, 8.75, -, -)"

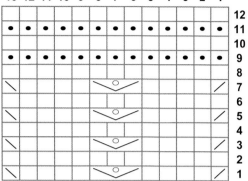

Stitch Pattern
Size - (-, -, -, 9.25, -)"

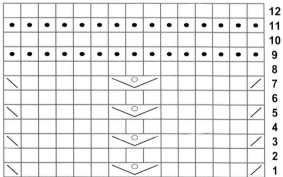

Stitch Pattern
Size - (-, -, -, -, 10.25)"

VALENSOLE
by Margaret Stauffacher

FINISHED MEASUREMENTS

7.5 (8.5, 9.5)" leg circumference × 8.75 (9.5, 10)" foot length, to fit US shoe sizes 7 (8–8.5, 9.5–10); meant to be worn with approx 10% negative ease

YARN

Static™ (fingering weight, 75% Superwash Wool, 25% Nylon; 437 yards/100g): Cameo 28485, 1 hank

NEEDLES

US 1 (2.25mm) 32" circular needles for Magic Loop technique or DPNs, or size to obtain gauge

US 0 (2.0mm) 32" circular needles for Magic Loop technique or DPNs, or one size smaller than size used to obtain gauge

NOTIONS

Yarn Needle
Stitch Markers
Scrap Yarn

GAUGE

28 sts and 40 rnds = 4" in Stockinette Stitch in the round, blocked

For pattern support, contact margaret@whimsynorth.com

Valensole

Notes:

Valensole, France is famous for its vibrant fields of lavender that stretch as far as the eye can see. The blossom stitch design that runs down the front of these socks mimics those majestic lavender fields.

Valensole Socks are shortie ankle-length socks that are worked in the round from the cuff down to the toes. They feature an afterthought heel and can be customized in length.

DL (Dip Left)
Insert RH needle into space 4 rows down and 2 sts to the left, wrap yarn around needle as if to knit, pulling yarn through into a big loop that will match tension of regular sts.

DR (Dip Right)
Insert RH needle into same space as DL, wrap yarn around needle as if to knit, pulling yarn through into a big loop that will match tension of regular sts.

3x2 Rib (in the round over a multiple of 5 sts)
Rnd 1: (K3, P2) to end.
Rep Rnd 1 for pattern.

DIRECTIONS

Cuff
With smaller needles, CO 50 (55, 60) sts using Long Tail Cast On, or other stretchy method. PM for BOR and join to work in the rnd, being careful not to twist sts.

Work 3x2 Rib until piece measures 1″ from CO edge.

Foot
Change to larger needles.
Setup Rnd: (K3, P2) 4 (4, 5) times, K3, P1, K to last st, P1.
Rep Setup Rnd three more times.

Rnd 1: (DL, K3, DR, P2) 4 (4, 5) times, DL, K3, DR, P1, K to last st, P1.
Rnd 2: (Sl1, K3, Sl1, P2) 4 (4, 5) times, Sl1, K3, Sl1, P1, K to last st, P1.
Rnd 3: (SKP, K1, K2tog, P2) 4 (4, 5) times, SKP, K1, K2tog, P1, K to last st, P1.
Rnd 4: (K3, P2) 4 (4, 5) times, K3, P1, K to last st, P1.
Rep Rnds 1–3 once more.

Insert Afterthought Heel
Next Rnd: (K3, P2) 4 (4, 5) times, K3, P1, with scrap yarn K to 1 st before BOR, transfer 25 (30, 30) scrap yarn sts back to LH needle, with working yarn K to last st, P1.

Foot Continued
Work Rnds 1–4 of Foot section until sock measures 5.5 (6.5, 7.5)″ from afterthought heel or 1.5″ shorter than desired length.

Toe
Change to smaller needles.

Size 7.5 (-, -)″ Only
Setup Rnd: K1, M1L, K24, PM, K1, M1L, K to end. 52 (-, -) sts.

Size - (8.5, -)″ Only
Setup Rnd: K1, M1L, K26, PM, K to end. - (56, -) sts.

Size - (-, 9.5)″ Only
Setup Rnd: K30, PM, K to end. - (-, 60) sts.

Resume All Sizes
Rnd 1: K all.
Rnd 2: K1, SSK, K to 3 sts before M, K2tog, K1, SM, K1, SSK, K to last 3 sts, K2tog, K1. 4 sts dec.
Rep Rnds 1–2 six more times. 24 (28, 32) sts.
Use Kitchener Stitch to graft toe closed.

Heel
Change to smaller needles.
Place sts on either side of scrap yarn onto needles, picking up 1 additional st at beginning and end of each side (4 total sts picked up). Remove scrap yarn. 54 (64, 64) sts.

Size 7.5 (-, -)″ Only
Setup Rnd: K1, M1L, K26, PM, K1, M1L, K to end. 56 (-, -) sts.

Size - (8.5, -)″ Only
Setup Rnd: (K1, SSK, K26, K2tog, K1, PM) two times. - (60, -) sts.

Size - (-, 9.5)″ Only
Setup Rnd: K32, PM, K to end. - (-, 64) sts.

Resume All Sizes
Rnd 1: K all.
Rnd 2: K1, SSK, K to 3 sts before M, K2tog, K1, SM, K1, SSK, K to last 3 sts, K2tog, K1. 52 (56, 60) sts.
Rep Rnds 1–2 seven more times. 24 (28, 32) sts.
Use Kitchener Stitch to graft heel closed.

Second Sock
Make second sock same as first.

Finishing
Weave in ends, wash, and block as desired.

Glossary
Common Stitches & Techniques for Socks

Visit our **Learning Center** to find tons of video and photo tutorials on sock techniques! knitpicks.com/learning-center/learn-to-knit-socks.

Slipped Stitches (Sl)
Always slip stitches purl-wise with yarn held to the wrong side of work, unless noted otherwise in the pattern.

Make 1 Left-Leaning Stitch (M1L)
Inserting LH needle from front to back, PU the horizontal strand between the st just worked and the next st, and K TBL.

Make 1 Right-Leaning Stitch (M1R)
Inserting LH needle from back to front, PU the horizontal strand between the st just worked and the next st, and K TFL.

Slip, Slip, Knit (SSK)
(Sl1 K-wise) twice; insert LH needle into front of these 2 sts and knit them together.

Centered Double Decrease (CDD)
Slip first and second sts together as if to work K2tog; K1; pass 2 slipped sts over the knit st.

Stockinette Stitch (in the round over any number of sts)
Rnd 1: Knit all sts.
Rep Rnd 1 for pattern.
Rev St st is the opposite—purl all sts.

1x1 Rib (in the round over an even number of sts)
Rnd 1: (K1, P1) to end of rnd.
Rep Rnd 1 for pattern.

2x2 Rib (in the round over a multiple of 4 sts)
Rnd 1: (K2, P2) to end of rnd.
Rep Rnd 1 for pattern.

Sock Measurement Guide

US Women's Shoe Size	4–6.5	7–9.5	10–12.5
Foot length	8–9"	9.25–10"	10.25–11"
Foot Circumference	7"	8"	9"
Sock Height	6.5"	7"	7.5"

US Men's Shoe Size	6–8.5	9–11.5	12–14
Foot length	9.25–10"	10.25–11"	11.25–12"
Foot Circumference	8"	9"	10"
Sock Height	7.5"	8"	8.5"

US Children's Shoe Size	10–13	1–3	4–6
	(Child)	(Youth)	(Youth)
Foot length	6.5–7.5"	7.75–8.5"	8.75–9.5"
Foot Circumference	6"	6.5"	7"
Sock Height	4.5"	5.5"	6.5"

Knitting in the Round (Magic Loop, Two Circulars, DPNs)
The **Magic Loop** technique uses one long circular needle to knit in the round around a small circumference. The **Two Circulars** technique uses two long circular needles to knit around a small circumference. Photo and video tutorials for these, plus using **DPNs** and 16" circular needles, can be found at knitpicks.com/learning-center/knitting-in-the-round.

Tubular Cast Ons
Stretchy cast on methods with a neat looking edge for 1x1 Rib; great for starting top-down socks. A tutorial for the **Long Tail Tubular Cast On** (which does not use scrap yarn) can be found at blog.knitpicks.com/long-tail-tubular-cast-on. A tutorial for the **standard Tubular Cast On** (which uses scrap yarn that gets removed at the end) can be found at tutorials.knitpicks.com/tubular-cast-on.

Abbreviations

approx	approximately		
BO	bind off		
BOR	beginning of round		
CN	cable needle		
C (1, 2...)	color (1, 2...)		
CC	contrast color		
CDD *(dec 2)*	centered double decrease *(see above)*		
CO	cast on		
cont	continue		
dec(s)	decrease(es)		
DPN(s)	double pointed needle(s)		
inc(s)	increase(s)		
K	knit		
K2tog *(dec 1)*	knit 2 stitches together		
K3tog *(dec 2)*	knit 3 stitches together		

KFB *(inc 1)*	knit into front and back of stitch
K-wise	knit-wise
LH	left hand
M	marker
M1 *(inc 1)*	make 1 stitch (work same as M1L)
M1L *(inc 1)*	make 1 left-leaning stitch *(see above)*
M1R *(inc 1)*	make 1 right-leaning stitch *(see above)*
MC	main color
P	purl
P2tog *(dec 1)*	purl 2 stitches together
P3tog *(dec 2)*	purl 3 stitches together
PM	place marker
PFB *(inc 1)*	purl into front and back of stitch

PSSO *(dec 1)*	pass slipped stitch over
PU	pick up
P-wise	purl-wise
rep	repeat
Rev St st	reverse stockinette stitch *(see above)*
RH	right hand
rnd(s)	round(s)
RS	right side
Sk	skip
SK2P *(dec 2)*	slip K-wise, knit 2 together, pass slipped stitch over
SKP *(dec 1)*	slip K-wise, knit, pass slipped stitch over
Sl	slip *(see above)*
SM	slip marker
SSK *(dec 1)*	slip, slip, knit these 2 stitches together *(see above)*

SSP *(dec 1)*	slip, slip, purl these 2 stitches together through back loop
SSSK *(dec 2)*	slip, slip, slip, knit these 3 stitches together (like SSK)
St st	stockinette stitch *(see above)*
st(s)	stitch(es)
TBL	through back loop
TFL	through front loop
tog	together
W&T	wrap & turn *(see next page)*
WE	work even
WS	wrong side
WYIB	with yarn in back
WYIF	with yarn in front
YO *(inc 1)*	bring yarn over needle from front up over to back

Jeny's Stretchy Slipknot Cast On

An extremely stretchy cast on method that does not require a long tail, great for starting top-down socks.
DIRECTIONS: Place a slip knot on needle. Make another slip knot with working yarn, but instead of placing it on needle, pull working yarn through slip knot, and place that loop on needle. Make sure this loop sits very close to previous st. Pull working yarn until new st is tight. Rep for all CO sts.

Long Tail Cast On

Fast and neat once you get the hang of it. A tutorial can be found at knitpicks.com/learning-center/learn-to-knit.

Judy's Magic Cast On

This method creates stitches coming out in opposite directions from a seamless center line, perfect for starting toe-up socks.
DIRECTIONS: Make a slip knot and place loop around one of the two needles; anchor loop counts as first st. Hold needles tog, with needle that yarn is attached to on top. In other hand, hold yarn so tail goes over index finger and yarn attached to ball goes over thumb. Bring tip of bottom needle over strand of yarn on finger (top strand), around and under yarn and back up, making a loop around needle. Pull loop snug. Bring top needle (with slip knot) over yarn tail on thumb (bottom strand), around and under yarn and back up, making a loop around needle. Pull loop snug. Cont casting on sts until desired number is reached; top yarn strand always wraps around bottom needle, and bottom yarn strand always wraps around top needle. A video tutorial can be found at knitpicks.com/video/judys-magic-cast-on.

Turkish Cast On

Another method that creates stitches coming out in opposite directions from a seamless center line, for toe-up socks.
DIRECTIONS: Make a slip knot and place it on one needle. Place two needles parallel, one on top of the other, with pointed ends facing the same direction and with slip knot loop on bottom needle. Take yarn and wrap around back, over top and back to front, looping around both needles. Make each loop to the right of the last loop. Rep until there are enough loops for half your needed CO sts, minus 1. Wrap yarn around top needle once more then bring yarn between needles. With another needle, knit sts across top needle, then knit sts across bottom needle. If using circulars, you can pull bottom needle through the loops so the loops are now on the cable and use it to knit the loops on top needle.

Stretchy Bind Off

Good basic option for binding off toe-up sock cuffs.
DIRECTIONS: K2, *insert LH needle into front of 2 sts on RH needle and knit them tog—1 st remains on RH needle. K1; rep from * until all sts have been bound off. A tutorial can be found at knitpicks.com/learning-center/sock-knitting-guide.

Jeny's Surprisingly Stretchy Bind Off (for 1x1 Rib)

A great option for binding off toe-up sock cuffs in 1x1 Rib.
DIRECTIONS: Reverse YO, K1, pass YO over; *YO, P1, pass YO and previous st over P1; reverse YO, K1, pass YO and previous st over K1; rep from * until 1 st is left, then break working yarn and pull it through final st to complete BO.

Tubular Bind Off (for 1x1 Rib)

Another good option for binding off toe-up sock cuffs in 1x1 Rib. A tutorial can be found at knitpicks.com/learning-center/tubular-bind-off.

Cables

Tutorials for different kinds of cables, including 1 over 1 and 2 over 2, with and without cable needles, can be found at knitpicks.com/learning-center/guides/cables.

Short Rows

There are several options for how to handle short rows, so you may see different suggestions/intructions in a pattern.

Wrap and Turn (W&T) (one option for Short Rows)

Work until the st to be wrapped. If knitting: Bring yarn to front, Sl next st P-wise, return yarn to back; turn work, and Sl wrapped st onto RH needle. Cont across row. If purling: Bring yarn to back of work, Sl next st P-wise, return yarn to front; turn work and Sl wrapped st onto RH needle. Cont across row. **Picking up Wraps:** Work to wrapped st. If knitting: Insert RH needle under wrap, then through wrapped st K-wise; K st and wrap tog. If purling: Sl wrapped st P-wise onto RH needle, use LH needle to lift wrap and place it onto RH needle; Sl wrap and st back onto LH needle, and P tog. A tutorial for W&T can be found at tutorials.knitpicks.com/short-rows-wrap-and-turn-or-wt.

German Short Rows (another option for Short Rows)

Work to turning point; turn. WYIF, Sl first st P-wise. Bring yarn over back of right needle, pulling firmly to create a "double stitch" on RH needle. If next st is a K st, leave yarn at back; if next st is a P st, bring yarn to front between needles. When it's time to work into double st, knit both strands tog. A video tutorial for German Short Rows can be found at knitpicks.com/video/german-short-rows.

Kitchener Stitch (also called Grafting)

Seamlessly join two sets of live stitches together.
DIRECTIONS: With an equal number of sts on two needles, break yarn leaving a tail approx four times as long as the row of sts, and thread through a blunt yarn needle. Hold needles parallel with WSs facing in and both needles pointing to the right. Perform Step 2 on the first front st, then Step 4 on the first back st, then continue from Step 1, always pulling yarn tightly so the grafted row tension matches the knitted fabric:
Step 1: Pull yarn needle K-wise through front st and drop st from knitting needle.
Step 2: Pull yarn needle P-wise through next front st, leaving st on knitting needle.
Step 3: Pull yarn needle P-wise through first back st and drop st from knitting needle.
Step 4: Pull yarn needle K-wise through next back st, leaving st on knitting needle.
Rep Steps 1–4 until all sts have been grafted together, finishing by working Step 1 through the last remaining front st, then Step 3 through the last remaining back st. Photo tutorials can be found at knitpicks.com/learning-center/learn-to-knit/kitchener.

THIS COLLECTION FEATURES

Hawthorne™
Multi, Speckle, Tonal & Kettle Dye
Fingering Weight
80% Fine Superwash Highland Wool, 20% Polyamide (Nylon)

Stroll™ Hand Painted
Stroll™ Tonal
Fingering Weight
75% Fine Superwash Merino Wool, 25% Nylon

Muse™
Fingering Weight
75% Superwash Merino Wool, 25% Nylon

Static™
Fingering Weight
75% Superwash Wool, 25% Nylon

Knit Picks®

View these beautiful
yarns and more at
www.KnitPicks.com

Knit Picks yarn is both luxe and affordable—a seeming contradiction
trounced! But it's not just about the pretty colors; we also care
deeply about fiber quality and fair labor practices, leaving you with
a gorgeously reliable product you'll turn to time and time again.